SPECTRUM®

Science

Grade 4

Spectrum®
An imprint of Carson-Dellosa Publishing LLC
P.O. Box 35665
Greensboro, NC 27425 USA

Published by Spectrum®
an imprint of Carson-Dellosa Publishing
Greensboro, NC

Spectrum®
An imprint of Carson-Dellosa Publishing LLC
P.O. Box 35665
Greensboro, NC 27425 USA

ISBN 978-1-4838-1168-0

06-011177811

Table of Contents

Chapter 4 Earth and Space Science

Chapter 5 Science and Technology

Chapter 6 Science in Personal and Social Perspectives

Chapter 7 History and Nature of Science

Lesson 1.1   The Scientific Method

skeptics: people who are slow to believe something; they ask many questions

solutions: answers to problems

proof: evidence or facts that show something to be true or correct

opinions: beliefs that are based experience, but that aren't necessarily proven to be true

hypothesis: a statement that is assumed to be true so that it can be tested

community: a group of people who are interested in the same thing

"Somewhere, something incredible is waiting to be known."—Carl Sagan, astronomer

What is the difference between a theory and a law?

Without science, we wouldn't know why water freezes, where the sun goes at night, or how our bodies fight disease. We have the answers, though, because someone was curious. Science always begins with a question.

Scientists want to find answers, but a good scientist doesn't stop working until he or she has the only possible answer. This is because the best scientists are **skeptics**. They never say they've solved a scientific problem if other possible **solutions** can be found. Science is based on **proof**. Statements that don't have proof are guesses or **opinions**.

The scientific method is a tool scientists use to prove things. It begins with a question. For example, "Do birds like one color more than another?"

The next step is to answer the question. At this point, it's okay to make a guess or have an opinion. You need something you can test. In the scientific method, your answer is called the **hypothesis**. A hypothesis is a simple statement that can be proven right or wrong. "Birds will eat more food from a red birdfeeder than a blue one" is a good hypothesis.

Now, you can test the hypothesis using experiments and observation. The tests must be designed carefully, though. If too many parts can be changed, it will be hard to tell why you got one result and not another.

If a hypothesis is unable to be proven, the next step is to make a new hypothesis and test it. If the experiments show that a hypothesis is proven, you'll still want to test it again. For example, maybe birds don't see color at all. Something else might have been attracting them to the feeders.

After a scientist finishes experimenting, he or she writes a conclusion. Then, the scientist shares the results with other scientists. The scientific **community** looks closely at the results. This step is very important in the scientific method. Other scientists will try to get the same results. Scientists double- and triple-check each other's work.

A hypothesis must be proven true many times before the scientific community accepts it as true. They're skeptics, remember? If a hypothesis makes it through lots and lots of testing, it will become a theory. A theory might still be proven wrong, but the chances are less. Theories that last for many, many years—and are never proven wrong—become scientific laws.

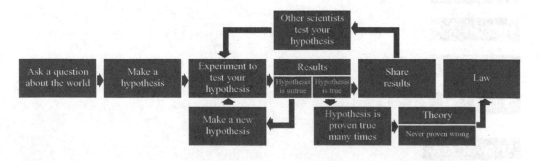

Circle the letter of the best answer to each question below.

1. A _hypothesis_ is a theory that has never been proven wrong.

   a. hypothesis

   b. solution

   c. law

   d. opinion

2. Which of the following would make a good hypothesis?

   a. Trees grow better in soil than sand.

   b. Do bees like some flowers better than others?

   c. I think apple juice tastes better than orange juice.

   d. Girls draw better than boys.

3. If an experiment fails to confirm your hypothesis, what is the next step?

   a. Find another solution.

   b. Make another hypothesis.

   c. Keep trying the same experiment.

   d. Use a different theory.

Write your answers on the lines below.

4. Explain why your answer to question 2 makes a good hypothesis.

   Not all trees grow in dessert, mostly trees need moisture, water where sand soaks moisture queckly soil have still water for some more days. So it will help tree to grow fast.

5. Why should a scientist always share the results of his or her experiments?

   Scientist always share results so that other can test their results and if proven right it will become theory in future.

6. Number the steps of the scientific method in the correct order.

   __2__ hypothesis

   __1__ question

   __3__ experiment

   __6__ law

   __5__ theory

   __4__ share results

Scientific Detectives

research: the act of studying, observing, or collecting in order to gain knowledge

investigator: someone who closely examines evidence to reach a conclusion

facts: things that really exist or happen; things that can be proven true

evidence: facts that help prove something

artifacts: simple objects, like tools, that show evidence of a human culture

conclusions: decisions made with careful thought

Police detectives use science, too. Forensic science is the use of science in solving crimes. Fingerprinting and DNA tests can help identify people. Clothing can be tested to show chemicals used in making explosives. All sorts of electronic devices have been invented to help investigate crimes.

How does a scientist do his or her job?

When most people think of a scientist, they picture someone in a lab wearing a white coat. Of course, some scientists do work in labs, but just as many are out in the world doing their **research**. They wear jeans and dig through the dirt hoping to discover the bones of a new dinosaur. They wear snowsuits, gloves, and goggles as they trudge through the snows of Antarctica. Scientists go wherever the search for an answer takes them.

Like a detective, a scientist is an **investigator**. He or she looks for clues that will help solve the mysteries of our world. The most useful clues to a scientist are **facts**. Gathering facts is probably a scientist's most important job. Scientists collect samples, make observations, and perform experiments to get the facts they need.

The main kind of investigation a scientist does changes from one kind of science to another. For example, an archaeologist studies human history. He or she spends many hours outdoors, sifting through layers of ground looking for **evidence**. Pieces of bone, chips of clay pots, or the remains of an ancient campfire are all good clues. Archaeologists collect these **artifacts**, study them closely, and draw **conclusions** about our human ancestors.

Observation is another important method of investigation. Zoology is the science of animal life on Earth. Much of a zoologist's work is observing animals in their natural habitats. Dian Fossey was a famous zoologist who studied gorillas. For years, she lived in the mountain forests of Rwanda. The gorillas went about their lives while Fossey quietly observed them and took notes. Then, like any good scientist would do, she shared her information with the world.

Collecting and observing are both good ways of getting clues, but the scientists aren't really in charge. Instead, they must be in the right place at the right time to get the facts they need. With an experiment, though, the scientist is in control. He or she designs an experiment to test exactly what needs to be known. Experimenting is an important scientific tool. It lets the scientist be in control.

Circle the letter of the best answer to each question below.

1. A biologist who wants to know what kind of fish live in a lake would

   a. design an experiment.

   b. make observations.

   c. collect all the fish from the lake.

   d. None of the above

2. Which of the following is an example of collecting evidence?

   a. a geologist gathering rocks from a mountainside

   b. a paleontologist cleaning fossils

   c. a botanist clipping leaves from plants

   d. All of the above

3. A physicist wants to know whether salt water boils more quickly than tap water, so she

   a. designs an experiment.

   b. collects evidence from the ocean.

   c. observes chefs cooking at a restaurant.

   d. asks a detective.

Write your answer on the lines below.

4. What kind of scientist would you want to be?

   I want to be an archaeologist, as I love to learn
   history and want to know about past.

Unifying Concepts and Processes

Do you think each branch of science uses only one method of investigation? Explain your answer.

No, there are different ways to investigate
and it depends on what we are investigating
example if we are investigating animal we will
observe, if we are finding chemicals in an object we
will do experiments, if we want to study past
we will gather facts and study them and past
will learn from it.

system: any group of living or nonliving things that combine to work together

organisms: living plants and animals

interconnected: needing and relying on each other

You are part of many systems. Attending school makes you part of the educational system. If you play a sport, your team is a system. You all work together to score points and win the game. Being a member of a club makes you part of a system, as well.

Like any system, an ecosystem works best when all its parts work together. When one part doesn't cooperate, the entire system suffers. When an ecosystem is damaged, though, it isn't just the plants and wild animals that suffer. The human beings who live there are affected, too, even if they caused the problem.

What is a system?

The United States government has three branches—the executive, judicial, and legislative. They work together to run our country. It's a great **system**. The post office has thousands of people working together. They move millions of letters around the country every day. It's a great system, too. These are both examples of people working together to get something done. A system doesn't have to be just people, though. A system is anything with parts that work together.

Systems are everywhere. Your body is a system. Its organs, muscles, and bones work together to keep you alive and moving around. In fact, all living things are systems. Plants have leaves, stems, and roots to keep them alive. Insects have antennae, wings, and legs that move them around.

Systems come in all shapes and sizes. Tiny bacteria have even tinier parts that work together. An ecosystem is all the plants and animals living together in one place. It's a system because all the **organisms** are **interconnected**. Earth is part of a solar system. The sun, planets, moons, comets, and asteroids are linked together by gravity.

Systems can even be part of other systems. Your body has a nervous system, a digestive system, and a skeletal system. Our planet has many different ecosystems, but they all work together as a planetary system called *Earth*.

Cars, pencil sharpeners, and vending machines are mechanical systems. Computers, video games, and stereos are electrical systems.

So what isn't a system? A sheet of paper isn't a system. It has only one part—the sheet of paper. Coffee mugs, benches, and keys aren't systems. They don't have parts working together.

The most important thing to remember about systems is that every part has a role. If you remove a part, the system won't work as well—or might not work at all. Take the laser out of a CD player, and you won't hear any music. A plant won't live for long if you cut off all its roots. A system depends on its parts. When all the parts are working, a system runs smoothly and efficiently—just the way it should.

Circle the letter of the best answer to the question below.

1. Which of the following is not a system?

   a. an ant colony

   b. a cactus

   c. a wooden board

   d. a radio

Write your answers on the lines below.

2. List three systems that were not already mentioned in this selection.

   Music industry   Joint family system   Library system,
   educational systems.

3. A key is not a system, but it is part of a system. Explain why.

   A key on its own can't do anything where as when its
   alinged to a lock it can open it, close it and then its workable.

4. Sometimes, one part of a system is more or less important than another. Think of a clock. What part could be missing, and still allow the clock to tell time? What part of a clock could not be missing? Explain your answers.

   If a clock has a glass on it and its broken one of its
   number is missing but the hands are there it will tell
   time. batteries and hands

5. Think of three systems that you are part of. What is your job in each system?

   a. family - mother and wife and daughter, sister

   b. education system - parent.

   c. Government → citizen.

Unifying Concepts and Processes

Some people think we don't need to worry about tiny insects or small fish becoming extinct. Scientists argue that every living thing, no matter how small it might be, needs to be protected. What do you think? Explain your answer.

   Yes, all living things should be protected as we all are
   inter dependent, if tiny insects or small fish become
   extinct, there will be disbalance in the ecosystem
   and we all cant survive

Under a Log

tally: to count and record

bar graph: a graph that shows rectangles of different lengths; used to make a comparison

Most of the insects that live among dead or rotting plant materials are decomposers. They help free stored energy from these materials. Over time, only small bits remain. These bits help nourish the next round of living things.

About 20% of woodland creatures make their homes in dead trees.

When eating wood, some termites make a ticking sound. Carpenter ants make more of a rustling sound as they eat wood.

What kinds of creatures make their homes under logs?

Austin and Alex walked to the far side of Alex's backyard. "How about this one?" asked Austin, pointing to a large, thick log that was covered with moss.

"That ought to work," replied Alex. He held up his notebook and pencil. "If you lift it up, I'll record what we see."

Austin lifted the log, and he and Alex peered beneath it. There was a great deal of scurrying as dozens of insects ran for cover. The boys tried to count the insects they could see, but quickly realized that many had already hidden themselves under a pile of dead leaves or another piece of wood.

"That didn't work out too well, did it?" asked Austin.

Alex shook his head. "Maybe we could try again and set the log on a sheet this time."

The second time the boys tried their project, they had better luck. They chose a medium-sized log and quickly set it on a large white sheet they had spread out in the yard. Alex counted the insects that were under the log. Austin recorded the insects that were on the log and on the sheet.

When they were finished, the boys put the log back exactly where they had found it. They gently shook out the sheet and went inside to **tally** their results. They spent the rest of the afternoon making a **bar graph** to use for their presentation to the class. They were sure that Ms. Yancy would give them an A+ for their project!

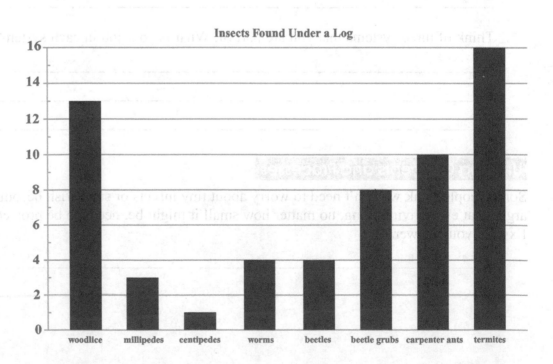

Insects Found Under a Log

Circle the letter of the best answer to the question below.

1. Which of the following is a question the boys might have been trying to answer when they began their project?

 a. Why do bugs live under logs?

 b. What causes tree limbs to die?

 c. What types of bugs live under logs?

 d. Why do ants, but not grasshoppers, live under logs?

Use the graph on page 12 to fill in the blanks below.

2. How many beetle grubs did Alex and Austin find? _8_____

3. The boys found the same number of _worms_ and _beetles_.

4. The boys found more millipedes than _centipedes_.

5. There were more _termites_ under the log than any other type of insect.

Write your answers on the lines below.

6. How did using a bar graph help Alex and Austin organize the information they collected?

With the help of bar graph they were able to write down the number of incests they found and how many of each count and therefore they were able to compare it easly

7. Why weren't the boys successful with the first log they tried?

The boys were successful with the first log because as soon as they picked the log the insects hid in leads and elsewhere and they were not able to record correctly.

8. How did they solve their problem?

This time they used the paper to keep the log on.

9. When the boys examined their bar graph, Alex said, "Now we know that more termites live under logs than any other type of insect." Explain why Alex cannot draw this conclusion.

_____

What's Next?

Bar graphs are only one kind of graphic organizer. Visit a library to find examples of other organizers, like pie charts, line graphs, or diagrams. Why are graphic organizers a helpful way to present information?

funnel: a hollow cone with a narrow tube at one end

inflate: to fill with air

variables: in an experiment, something that can be changed

A mixture of baking soda and vinegar has many practical uses. The combination can clean out a clogged drain. It can be used to polish coins or kill weeds in the cracks of cement. Some people wash their hair with it, and others use it to get pet stains out of carpeting.

Baking soda and vinegar are often used to help model volcanoes "erupt" in science fair projects. Just add a little red or orange food coloring to the mixture, and it looks like hot lava is bubbling out of the volcano.

Is there more than one way to inflate a balloon?

Annie rummaged through the kitchen cupboards. "Here it is!" she said, setting the orange box on the counter.

"Great," said Kimiko. She checked the list she was holding. "Baking soda was the only material we were missing. We're ready to get started."

Annie held out a plastic soda bottle. "How much vinegar do I need?"

"About half a cup," replied Kimiko. As Annie poured the vinegar into the bottle, Kimiko used a **funnel** to put a tablespoon of baking soda into a balloon.

"Are you ready?" Kimiko asked Annie. Annie nodded, and Kimiko carefully fitted the balloon over the opening to the soda bottle. Annie held up the top of the balloon so that the powder inside would fall into the bottle. As the specks of baking soda hit the vinegar, it began to fizz. Tiny bubbles began filling the bottle. As the girls watched, the balloon started to **inflate**.

"Perfect!" cheered Annie. "That is exactly what we wanted to happen. When the baking soda mixed with the vinegar, it caused a chemical reaction to take place. Carbon dioxide was released. It's a gas, so it caused the balloon to fill."

"Now we need to experiment with some **variables**," said Kimiko. "We need to change one part of our experiment and see what kind of results we get. I wonder what would happen if we used an acid other than vinegar. What about orange juice?"

"We have a brand-new carton in the refrigerator," said Annie. "I'd also like to try using yeast. Sometimes, I help my dad bake bread. The first step is to add yeast to some warm water. The way it bubbles up reminded me of the baking soda. I'm curious to see what happens when we add it to vinegar. Will the yeast be able to inflate the balloon, too?"

"Sounds good to me," said Kimiko. "Let's just remember that we can change only one variable at a time. Otherwise, we won't know which part of the experiment has caused a change in our results."

"Got it," said Annie. She opened the refrigerator and pulled out the juice and a small packet of yeast. "Let's see what happens next!"

Circle the letter of the best answer to each question below.

1. What caused the balloon to inflate when Annie and Kimiko did their experiment?

   a. vinegar

   b. baking soda

   c. a chemical reaction

   d. Not enough information is given.

2. Which of the following could be a variable?

   a. the size of the balloon

   b. the liquid in the bottle

   c. the powder placed in the balloon

   d. All of the above

vinegar
vinegar

Write your answers on the lines below.

3. Why do you think Kimiko put the baking soda into the balloon? What probably would have happened if she had put it into the bottle and then put the balloon on the bottle afterward?

   The chemical reaction will happen as soon as we put baking soda in the vinegar. if she ut it after words it might not be the same results and the balloon might have not inflated.

4. Explain why only one variable at a time should be changed.

   Because if we change to many at a time we will not come to know which variable has changed the results

5. The next time Kimiko and Annie do the experiment, they are going to use baker's yeast. Write the hypothesis you think they plan to test.

   As yeast will be added to vinegar, with chemical reaction the yeast will start bubbling and will help the balloon to inflate.

6. Name two other substances, besides orange juice and baker's yeast, that Kimiko and Annie could test.

   _____   _____

stable: not easily changing chemical or physical states

result: effect; something that happens because of something else

Charles Goodyear spent most of his adult life very poor. He put any money he had into his scientific research. When he died, he was $200,000 in debt. He had the rights to his invention, but he didn't earn much money from it during his life.

No one in Goodyear's family worked at the Goodyear Company that became well known for selling tires. The company was just named to honor Charles Goodyear and his discovery.

Goodyear was known for making all kinds of things out of rubber. He wore rubber clothing, had rubber business cards, and even had his portrait painted on a piece of rubber.

Who made rubber the useful material that it is today?

If you look around, you can probably spot at least a few things that are made of rubber—a ball, the bottoms of your sneakers, the wheels of a car. Without the patience and work of Charles Goodyear, none of them would have been possible.

Rubber begins as the sticky sap of a tropical tree. In the early 1800s, people thought that this waterproof material was the wave of the future. They were eager to use things made of rubber. It wasn't long, though, before they realized that rubber wasn't as useful as it first seemed. When it got cold out, rubber froze and became brittle. When it was hot, rubber melted and turned into a gooey mess. Suddenly, no one wanted to use rubber products anymore.

Charles Goodyear was fascinated with rubber. He was sure that there was a way to make it **stable** and easy to use. He began to work with the rubber gum, kneading it and rolling it out. He experimented with it by adding different materials. He thought that he might be able to add a powder to the rubber that would keep it from getting so sticky in the heat. The first type of powder he added was called *magnesia*. He made shoes from this rubber, but they melted. Goodyear needed to try something else.

The next time, he decided to experiment with magnesia and something called *quicklime*. He boiled the mixture and got a slightly better **result**. However, he found that when this rubber touched even a mild acid, like lemon juice or vinegar, it was ruined.

Others might have given up, but Goodyear knew he could find a solution to the problem. He added nitric acid and found that the rubber seemed smoother and drier. He was sure that he had made a better product. Sadly, he was wrong. The mailbags he made of this new rubber melted in the heat, too.

After years of work, Goodyear learned that sulfur might help dry out the rubber. He made the mixture and kept on experimenting with it. One day, a piece of it accidentally dropped onto a hot stovetop. Instead of melting, it turned tough and leathery. When the mixture of rubber gum and sulfur was heated at a high temperature, it became stable. Goodyear had finally found a solution!

Circle the letter of the best answer to each question below.

1. Which of the following could have been one of Goodyear's hypotheses?

    a. What will make rubber a more stable product?

    b. Adding sulfur to rubber will make the rubber stable.

    c. Why isn't rubber stable at high or low temperatures?

    d. Rubber comes from the sap of a tree in Brazil.

2. By adding powder to rubber gum, Goodyear hoped that

    a. he could use rubber as a sort of cement.

    b. he could show that rubber was not a useful product.

    c. the rubber would freeze more easily.

    d. the rubber would become less sticky.

3. Rubber that is stable

    a. does not easily melt or freeze.

    b. would melt on a hot summer day.

    c. would freeze at temperatures below 32°F.

    d. Both b and c

Write your answers on the lines below.

4. What problem did Goodyear's discovery solve?

    _____

    _____

5. Why was patience an important quality for Goodyear to have as a scientist?

    _____

    _____

6. What happened when one of Goodyear's early mixtures came in contact with an acid?

    _____

    _____

7. Why were experiments a good choice for Goodyear's scientific investigation?

    _____

    _____

A Weighty Matter

mass: the amount of matter something has, measured in kilograms

volume: the amount of space something takes up, measured in cubes

density: the amount of matter there is in a given space or area

White dwarf stars are stars that have died. An average-sized white dwarf is about the size of Earth but weighs more than 100,000 times as much as Earth.

What's the difference between mass and weight?

Fill a cardboard box with packing peanuts, and you won't have any problem lifting it. Fill the same box with sand, and you'll struggle to get it off the ground. The box didn't get any bigger, but it got a lot heavier.

Scientists use the word **mass** to talk about weight. Mass is the number of kilograms an object weighs on Earth. The problem with weight is that it's based on gravity. A scale measures how strongly Earth's gravity pulls on something. On another planet, the gravity will be stronger or weaker than on Earth, so an object's weight will be different. Mass tells scientists the number of kilograms something has, no matter where it is in the universe. As long as you're on Earth, though, mass and weight are basically the same thing.

An object's mass has little to do with its **volume**. Mass is based on **density**. For example, a one-inch cube of iron has a lot more mass than a one-inch cube of oxygen. This is because there are many more atoms in the cube of iron. Everything is made of atoms, but how closely atoms are packed together—how dense they are—changes from one thing to another.

Think of the cardboard box filled with packing peanuts as the cube of oxygen. Each packing peanut is one atom. The cardboard box filled with sand is the cube of iron. Each grain of sand is one atom, too. The box holds many more grains of sand than it does packing peanuts. The volume is the same, but the mass is very different.

Each atom has mass. An object's mass is the total weight of all its atoms combined. The more atoms something has, the more it will weigh. Gas is less dense than a solid because a gas's atoms are spread farther apart. The space needed to hold a pound of helium is much bigger than the space needed for a pound of gold.

The planets in our solar system are good places to see why mass depends mostly on density, not volume. For example, Jupiter is more than 1,000 times bigger than Earth, but its mass is only about 300 times greater. This is because Earth is made mostly of rock. Jupiter is made mostly of gas. If Jupiter were the same size as Earth, Jupiter would weigh much less than Earth because gases are always less dense than solids. A planet's mass depends more on density than size.

Circle the letter of the best answer to each question below.

1. What is volume?

    a. the amount something weighs

    b. the amount of mass something has

    c. the amount of space something takes up

    d. Both a and b

2. Weight and mass are the same thing

    a. in space.

    b. on Earth.

    c. in gases.

    d. when measuring volume.

3. Block A and Block B have the same volume. If Block A is less dense than Block B, which statement is true?

    a. Blocks A and B have the same mass.

    b. Block A is smaller than Block B.

    c. Block B has more mass than Block A.

    d. None of the above

Write your answers on the lines below.

4. Explain why your weight would be different if you traveled to another planet.

    _____

    _____

5. Blocks A and B have the same volume but are made of different materials. Block B weighs five times more than Block A. What does this tell you about Block B's material?

    _____

    _____

What's Next?

Do some research on the Internet or at a library to find out how much you would weigh on another planet.

Review

Circle the letter of the best answer to each question below.

1. A biologist gathers samples of four different kinds of mushrooms growing in the forest. This is an example of

   a. scientific observation.

   b. an experiment.

   c. collecting information.

   d. All of the above

2. Alex and Austin looked under another log and saw two garter snakes. What conclusion can be drawn from the boys' observation?

   a. All garter snakes live under logs.

   b. Garter snakes prefer living under logs.

   c. Garter snakes always travel in pairs.

   d. Two garter snakes were found under the log the boys lifted.

3. Caroline wants to know if a piece of chalk will dissolve in liquid. She places chalk in water, pop, orange juice, and milk. In this experiment, the liquids are

   a. variables.

   b. hypotheses.

   c. observations.

   d. methods.

4. Blocks A and B are the exact same size, but Block B is much heavier. This tells you that

   a. Block B has a greater volume.

   b. the molecules in Block B are packed more tightly together.

   c. Block B is made of a denser material.

   d. Both b and c

5. In Annie and Kimiko's experiment, why did the balloon inflate?

   a. because vinegar is an acid

   b. because yeast makes bread rise

   c. because mixing baking soda and vinegar creates a gas

   d. because baking soda is dry

Write your answers on the lines below.

6. Why do you think scientists use different methods of investigation?

_____

_____

7. The diagram below is missing three of the steps in the scientific method. Put the following steps where they belong: hypothesis, question, share results

_____ → _____ → experiment → _____ → theory → law

8. Explain why a bicycle is a system.

_____

9. Give two examples of things that are not systems.

_____ _____

10. Why was Charles Goodyear a good scientist?

_____

_____

11. Explain why weight and mass are not exactly the same thing.

_____

_____

Write **true** or **false** next to each statement below.

12. _____ A hypothesis is a scientific question.

13. _____ All scientists work in labs.

14. _____ Experiments are good scientific tools because the scientist is in control.

15. _____ A bar graph is a simple way to compare data.

16. _____ Charles Goodyear invented tires.

17. _____ Volume is the amount of space something takes up.

Lesson 2.1   On the Move

motion: the act of moving from one place to another

force: the push or pull that can move an object at rest or cause it to stop moving

acceleration: an increase in the rate of speed

reaction: a response; something that happens as a result of something else

equal: the same as

Newton was made a knight by Queen Anne in 1705. From that time on, he was known as Sir Isaac Newton.

Newton was in college when a terrible, deadly illness, called the *plague*, struck London. His university closed for two years. Newton continued his studies at home by himself.

What are the three laws of motion?

Look around you. Things are in **motion** everywhere. Curtains blow in the breeze, a car drives by, a child bounces on a trampoline. Isaac Newton, one of history's most famous scientists, saw motion all around him, too. He came up with three laws of motion.

The first law says that things tend to keep doing what they are doing. If you roll a ball across the ground, it will keep on rolling in a straight line. What happens if you place a shoe in front of the ball? The ball will stop. An object in motion (the ball) will stay in motion unless it is acted on by a **force** (the shoe).

Now, picture a ball sitting in the middle of a field. Will it start moving on its own? Of course not! It is an object at rest. It will stay at rest unless it is acted on, by a person kicking it, for example. The first law says that an object at rest (the ball) will stay at rest unless it is acted on by a force (a person kicking it).

The second law states that when you apply force to something, it will change its speed or direction. Imagine that a hockey player has just hit a puck. It is zipping across the ice at a certain speed when you give it a hard whack with your stick. Now, the puck is heading in a different direction and moving even more quickly.

The second law of motion also says that it takes more force to move or stop something with a large mass than something with less mass. It requires less force to push a golf ball across a table than a bowling ball. If you use the same amount of force when you push both balls, the golf ball will have greater **acceleration**, meaning it will speed up faster, than the bowling ball.

The third law of motion says that for every action there is an equal and opposite **reaction**. When a force is applied to something, it will push back with an **equal** force. When you hammer a nail into the wall, the nail pushes back on the hammer. You can feel the nail's force when the hammer bounces back toward you.

Isaac Newton died more than 250 years ago, but he was a talented scientific thinker. His ideas of motion are still used today.

Read each item below. If it is an example of the first law of motion, write **1** on the line. If it is an example of the second law, write **2**. If it is an example of the third law, write **3**.

1. _____ When you sit on a chair, you place the force of your weight on it. The chair pushes back at you with equal force.

2. _____ Caleb is skateboarding down the street.

3. _____ A book falls down and knocks over a lamp.

4. _____ A rocket blasts off from Earth. The force of its engines pushes against the ground, and the ground pushes back up against the rocket with equal force.

5. _____ Sara and Eduardo are building a snowman. Sara pushes a small snowball across the yard. Eduardo pushes a huge snowball. Sara uses much less force to push her snowball.

6. _____ An apple is sitting in a bowl.

Fill in the blanks in the sentences below with words from the box.

rest	force	reaction

7. For every action, there is an equal and opposite _____ .

8. An object at rest will tend to stay at _____ .

9. _____ is something that can move an object or cause it to stop moving.

Write your answers on the lines below.

10. What will happen when force is applied to something that is moving? Give an example to illustrate your answer.

_____

_____

_____

11. You are pulling an empty wagon. Your father is pulling a cart filled with firewood. You and your father are using the same amount of force. Which will be moving faster, the cart or the wagon? Why?

_____

_____

_____

The Conservation of Matter

matter: something that takes up space and has mass

states: stages or conditions of matter, especially solid, liquid, and gas

molecule: the smallest piece of something before it's broken into individual atoms

atoms: smallest pieces of matter; they can exist alone or combine to form molecules

chemical: referring to the structure or makeup of matter and substances

The best-known states of matter are solid, liquid, and gas. Others have been discovered, though. Plasmas are similar to gases, but the atoms have more energy. When gas inside a fluorescent light is charged with electricity, it becomes plasma. The Northern Lights and neon signs are plasmas, also.

Another state of matter was first discovered in 1995. It's called the *Bose-Einstein condensate*. This state of matter occurs when certain elements become so cold, their atoms almost stop moving.

When you burn a log, where does it go?

Flour, sugar, eggs, milk, baking powder, salt, and vanilla. Mix them all together in a bowl, put the mixture in a pan, and bake it. When the ingredients come out of the oven, they've become a cake. It doesn't look anything like eggs, milk, or sugar anymore. Where did the ingredients go? They haven't gone anywhere—they've just changed shape.

In a similar way, **matter** often appears to change forms or even disappear altogether. Think of a puddle of water on the sidewalk. After a few hours in the hot sun, it disappears. The water didn't really disappear, though. It changed **states**, turning from a liquid into a gas and floating away. *Conservation of matter* means that the amount of matter does increase or decrease, it just changes.

Water in the air is a gas, but it's made of the same matter that filled the puddle. Whether ice, liquid, or steam, each **molecule** has two hydrogen **atoms** and one oxygen atom. Water is always H_2O, no matter what state it's in.

Three states of matter are solid, liquid, and gas. Heat or pressure can change matter from one state to another. These are only physical changes, though. Ice cubes look nothing like steam, but they are both made of the same molecules—H_2O. A **chemical** change is different. It's when one kind of matter becomes another kind because its molecules change. They break apart, losing some of their atoms and taking on new ones.

When you burn a piece of wood, it goes through a chemical change. Like the cake, a piece of wood contains many different ingredients, or matter. The wood is made of lots of different atoms and molecules.

Atoms are extremely small, but they still have mass. When you weigh something, you are really weighing all of its atoms and molecules. After you burn a piece of wood, you end up with a pile of ash. The mass of the ash is much less than that of the wood. Where did the rest of it go?

When wood burns, chemical changes take place. The matter in the wood becomes different matter. It doesn't just change states. Most of the solid matter in the wood changes into gases and smoke. If you could capture the smoke and gases and weigh them along with the ash, it all would weigh the same amount as the original piece of wood. Matter is never destroyed, it just changes form.

Circle the letter of the best answer to each question below.

1. What are three states of matter?

   a. ice, water, and steam

   b. hot, warm, and cold

   c. atoms, molecules, and matter

   d. solid, liquid, and gas

2. When boiling water turns to steam, the water has

   a. gone through a chemical change.

   b. gone through a physical change.

   c. melted.

   d. All of the above

3. Two apples are placed on a balance, one on each side. Each apple is sealed inside a jar. The balance reads level, so you know that the mass of each apple and its jar is equal to the other. A flame is placed underneath the apple on the left. Soon, it becomes shriveled and much smaller than the apple on the right. How does the balance read now?

   a. The right side is heavier.

   b. The left side is heavier.

   c. The balance is still level.

   d. Not enough information is given.

Write your answers on the lines below.

4. Explain why you chose your answer to question 3.

   _____

   _____

5. List two things that can cause matter to change states.

   _____   _____

6. When an oxygen atom is added to H_2O, or water, you get H_2O_2, or hydrogen peroxide.

   This is an example of a _____ change.

Molecules in Motion

concentrated:
gathered together in
one body or shape

In the early 1800s,
Robert Brown looked
through a microscope
at tiny grains of
pollen floating in
water. He noticed that
no matter how long he
left the water sitting
still, the pollen never
quit moving. What
was making the grains
move? Nearly one
hundred years later,
Albert Einstein used
Brown's observation
to prove that atoms
and molecules exist.
Einstein showed that
the pollen never
stopped moving
because something
even smaller—water
molecules—pushed
the grains around.

How can you prove molecules are moving if you can't see them?

Mr. Harris walked to the sink and filled a glass with water. He held the glass up so the students could see it. "Is this water moving?" he asked.

"Yes," Tanika answered. "I can see it moving in the glass because your hand isn't very steady."

Mr. Harris laughed. He set the glass on a shelf. "How about now?"

"It was moving when you were holding it," Thomas explained. "You just set it down, so the water probably hasn't totally stopped moving yet."

Mr. Harris agreed. "Let's just leave it there for a while, then."

The next day, Mr. Harris stood by the sink again. He pointed to the glass, which had sat undisturbed for almost 24 hours. "Is this water moving now?" Mr. Harris asked.

"No way," Luiz answered. "No one's touched it since yesterday."

Mr. Harris opened a drawer and removed a small bottle. Without touching the glass, he added three drops of green food coloring from the bottle to the water. The drops slowly drifted to the bottom of the glass. "As long as this water isn't moving, those drops should just stay at the bottom of the glass, right?" Mr. Harris asked. Everyone agreed. "Let's leave it alone," Mr. Harris said, "and check again tomorrow."

The next day, the first thing the students noticed was the green water. The food coloring had moved from where it was **concentrated** at the bottom of the glass. Now, it was spread evenly throughout the water.

Mr. Harris reminded the students that no one had touched the water for two days. He explained that molecules are always in motion. No matter how long the water sat without moving, its molecules kept bouncing around— even though you couldn't see them. The molecules of the food coloring stayed clumped together at first. All the molecules in the glass were in motion, though. The water molecules and food coloring molecules were soon mixed together.

"The green water," Mr. Harris pointed out, "is our proof of molecules in motion."

Circle the letter of the best answer to each question below.

1. Atoms and molecules are _____ in motion.

    a. sometimes

    b. always

    c. rarely

    d. almost always

2. Mr. Harris let the water sit still for two days because

    a. he wanted it to be room temperature.

    b. he needed time to buy food coloring.

    c. he wanted only molecules to be moving in the glass.

    d. he needed some of the water to evaporate.

3. The water appeared motionless to the students because

    a. molecules are too small to see.

    b. the glass was sitting on a high shelf.

    c. the water didn't have any color yet.

    d. it was very cold.

4. Which of these variables do you think would most likely change the results of the experiment?

    a. using red food coloring instead of green

    b. using bottled water instead of tap water

    c. using ice instead of water

    d. using a different sized glass

Write your answer on the lines below.

5. In your own words, explain why the food coloring moved around in the glass.

_____

_____

_____

displaces: pushes aside, or takes the place of

buoyancy force: the force with which water pushes up on an object

dissolves: mixes with a liquid so that the liquid is the same throughout

Archimedes was an inventor and mathematician in ancient Greece. He was the first person to explain buoyancy force and how it worked. The story goes that he discovered this principle one day when he got into the bath and some water flowed over the side. He leapt out, shouting "Eureka!" which means "I found it!" in Greek.

The Dead Sea, on the border of Israel and Jordan, is the second saltiest body of water on the planet. In fact, it's hard to swim in the Dead Sea because the buoyancy force is so high. The Dead Sea is almost ten times saltier than the ocean.

Why do some things float while others sink?

Lie on your back in a swimming pool, and you'll float. Why don't you sink to the bottom? When an object is put into water, it **displaces**, or pushes aside, some of the water. Imagine you placed a block of wood that weighed two ounces into a glass of water. The wood would displace two ounces of water. **Buoyancy force** is the force of the water that was pushed aside. This force pushes up on the object and causes it to float.

If something is very dense, the atoms and molecules are packed together tightly. Metal, like iron, is denser than wood. A piece of iron would weigh more than a piece of wood of the same size. If you put it in the glass of water, it would sink, because it is denser than the water.

Do the following experiment to see buoyancy in action:

- First, gather a tablespoon, an empty plastic soda bottle, a pair of scissors, an empty spice jar, a wooden spoon with a long handle, and a container of table salt.

- With the help of an adult, cut the neck off the pop bottle and fill it about two-thirds full with water. Fill about one-third of the spice jar with water. Screw on the lid tightly and place it in the pop bottle. The spice jar will slowly sink to the bottom.

- Now, take out the jar and add about four tablespoons of salt to the water in the pop bottle. Stir it around until it **dissolves**.

- Place the jar back in the bottle. Has anything changed? Try stirring in another four tablespoons of salt. Does that make a difference?

- At some point, the jar will begin to float. The more salt you add, the higher the jar will float. Do you know why? The salt makes the water denser, or heavier. That means that it can push back on the jar with greater buoyancy force. The more force there is pushing up on the jar, the better it will float.

Circle the letter of the best answer to the question below.

1. Devonne had a glass marble and a grape that were about the same size. He placed each one in a glass of water. The marble sank, and the grape floated. This is because

   a. the grape was denser than the marble.

   b. the marble was denser than the grape.

   c. he used freshwater.

   d. he used salt water.

Write **true** or **false** next to each statement below.

2. _____ If an object weighs 9 pounds, it will displace 9 pounds of water.

3. _____ The saltier water is, the more easily things will float in it.

4. _____ The force of buoyancy causes objects to sink.

5. _____ All objects have the same density.

Write your answers on the lines below.

6. When you get into a bathtub full of water, the level of water rises. Explain why this happens.

   _____

   _____

7. Imagine you wanted to know which two substances was denser. If both objects were the same size, how could you figure this out?

   _____

   _____

8. In the experiment, why do you need to fill the spice jar partway with water?

   _____

Unifying Concepts and Processes

Name another variable you could use in the experiment. Explain why changing this variable could have an effect on the experiment's results.

   _____

   _____

chemical reaction: the chemical change that occurs when two or more molecules interact

ignite: to catch on fire

emit: to give off or send out

particles: very small pieces

flammable: something that easily catches fire or burns quickly

Whenever atoms of oxygen combine with molecules of another substance, it's called *oxidation*. Oxidation is a common chemical reaction. Fire is an example of rapid, or fast, oxidation. The excited molecules of a heated fuel quickly join with oxygen atoms in the air. This chemical reaction produces fire. Rust is an example of slow oxidation. Iron atoms in a piece of metal join with oxygen molecules. This chemical reaction takes much longer and produces iron oxide—better known as *rust*.

What is fire?

One of humankind's greatest achievements was controlling fire. It frightened away dangerous animals. It cooked meat to kill the germs that made people ill. Heat allowed human beings to move where it was otherwise too cold to live. Fire lit up the night so human beings had more useful hours each day.

Of course, fire is dangerous, too. Wildfires burn thousands of acres each year. Fires have damaged or destroyed many homes and buildings. Whether it's burning safely in a fireplace, roaring through the woods, or flickering at the top of a candle, all fire is basically the same.

Fire is a **chemical reaction** that needs three things: fuel, heat, and oxygen. If one of them is missing, a fire won't **ignite**.

Fuel is anything that burns. Wood, cloth, coal, and wax are solid fuels. Kerosene and gasoline are liquid fuels. Propane is a gas that is burned.

When a solid fuel burns, it goes through a chemical change. The solid matter changes into gases that begin floating away. These hot gases rise and mix with oxygen in the air. If the gases are hot enough, or if a spark is added, the mixture ignites and you have fire.

Look closely at a burning candle, and you will see a space between the wick and the flame. The candle's fuels—the wick and the wax—burn and **emit** gases. In the air above the fuel, the gases mix with oxygen and create a flame. It hovers just above the fuel.

Flames are the visible parts of fire. Often, flames are yellow or orange. Their color comes from glowing **particles** of unburned carbon, a dust called *soot*. Soot is very light. Gases rising from a solid fuel carry *soot* into the flame's heat.

When there's no soot, a flame will usually be blue. If you've ever seen the flame inside a furnace, then you've seen a blue flame. Natural gas doesn't have soot because it isn't a solid.

All fire is hot, but the tip of a flame is its hottest spot. Heat streams out of the peak of a flame. This hot spot is invisible, and it rises higher than the part of the flame you can see. This is why you should never put anything **flammable** near an open flame.

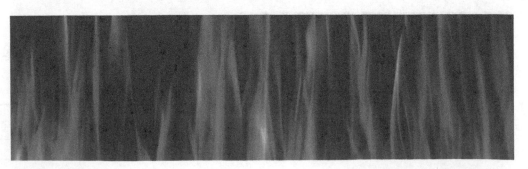

Circle the letter of the best answer to each question below.

1. What three things are needed to make fire?

   a. oxygen, wood, and gas

   b. heat, fuel, and oxygen

   c. fuel, fire, and wood

   d. gas, fire, and fuel

2. Flames are often yellow or orange because

   a. they are hot.

   b. they are burning kerosene.

   c. gas is mixing with oxygen.

   d. there is soot in the flame.

3. The hottest part of a flame is

   a. in its center.

   b. where it glows the brightest.

   c. at its tip.

   d. in the space between the fuel and the flame.

Write your answers on the lines below.

4. Fire is a _____.

5. Explain why some flames are blue.

   _____

   _____

6. Why is fire considered an example of oxidation?

   _____

   _____

7. _____ and _____ are the fuels in a candle.

circuit: the complete path of an electric current

current: a stream of electric charges

Devices that use batteries instead of cords contain circuits, too. Batteries become part of the circuit. The circuit isn't closed, though, until you turn the device on. Then, power flows through the device, through the batteries, and back into the device.

Electricity is measured in amps, ohms, and volts. If you think about water flowing through a pipe, you can get a rough idea of what these measurements mean. Amps measure how fast the water flows. Ohms measure how wide the pipe is. Volts measure the water's pressure.

What is an electrical circuit?

Electricity flows through wires running inside the walls of your home. These wires bring power to lights, TVs, and every other device connected to your home's electrical system. What you might not know is that a device's power cord does more than just bring electricity in. It carries electricity back out, too. This is because electricity that's used to power things must travel in a **circuit**.

Electricity has to be moving to work. Imagine water flowing under a waterwheel. The wheel turns only if the water is moving. Devices work in a similar way. Electricity must flow through a device to give it power. A circuit, or loop, keeps electricity on the move.

Before the walls of your home were finished, an electrician ran wires from the fuse box to each of the rooms. Then, he or she connected the ends of these wires back to the fuse box. The electrician was creating electrical circuits to bring power to each room.

Electricity enters your home at the fuse box. Then, it travels along a wire until it reaches the outlet in a room. When you plug in a power cord and turn on a device, electricity begins flowing. It goes from the outlet, through the cord, and into the device. The electrical **current** doesn't stop there, though. It heads right back out of the device. The power cord holds a second wire that brings electricity back to the outlet. Then, wires inside the wall run electricity back to the fuse box, where the circuit is completed.

If there's a break anywhere along a circuit, electricity will stop flowing. This is called an *open circuit*. When a circuit is closed, electricity is able to flow through the entire loop. When you flip on a light switch, you cause wires inside the wall to touch. The connected wires complete, or close, the circuit that runs from the switch, to the lamp, and back to the switch. When you flip the switch off, you disconnect the wires. This opens the circuit, and electricity can no longer flow through it.

Electricity that isn't in a circuit, like lightning, can't be controlled. Circuits let human beings make use of this powerful energy source.

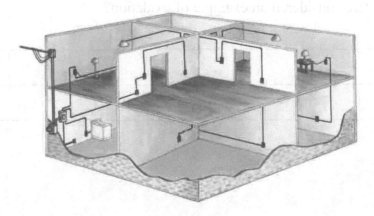

Use the following diagram to answer the questions below.

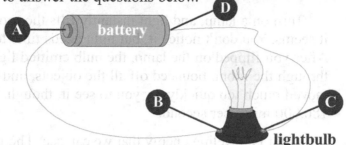

Circle the letter of the best answer to each question below.

1. If the light bulb produces light, you know the circuit is

    a. open.

    b. closed.

    c. current.

    d. None of the above

2. If you disconnect the wire at _____, you will have an open circuit.

    a. connection A

    b. connection C

    c. connection D

    d. any of the connections

3. The battery is

    a. providing electricity.

    b. part of the circuit.

    c. part of the light bulb.

    d. Both a and b

Unifying Concepts and Processes

A filament is the small wire inside a light bulb that produces light. The filament gets hot and glows when electricity runs through it. Look inside a burned-out bulb, and you will see that the filament is broken. Why do you think a bulb no longer works once the filament breaks?

_____

_____

_____

The Nature of Light

electromagnetic radiation: traveling waves of energy, including x-rays, radio waves, and light energy

spectrum: range

sources: places where things begin

reflect: to send back waves of light

prisms: objects that bend light and break it into the colors of the rainbow

absorb: to take in or swallow up

light-years: measurements used for the distances to stars; one light year is the distance light travels in a year, or about 5.879 trillion miles

Waves in the spectrum are measured by length. Human beings can't see wavelengths that are longer than red or shorter than violet. For example, ultraviolet light has a shorter wavelength than violet, so you can't see it.

Ultraviolet light is the part of sunlight that causes sunburns and skin cancer. The ozone layer protects Earth from getting too much of the sun's ultraviolet light.

How does light create the world around us?

Turn on a lamp, and light instantly fills the room—or at least that's how it seems. You don't notice it, but light needs time to move through space. After you flipped on the lamp, the bulb emitted light. This light traveled through the room, bounced off all the objects, and then entered your eye. It moved much too quickly for you to see it, though. Light moves at about 186,000 miles per second.

Light is traveling energy that we can see. There are many other types of energy: radio waves, microwaves, and x-rays are all different forms of **electromagnetic radiation**. The electromagnetic **spectrum** is the range of all the energy waves around us. Different types of waves have different properties. Some waves, like radio waves, can go through solid objects. Some can be dangerous to human beings, like UV waves from the sun. Light is the special kind of energy that our eyes can detect.

The sun, a light bulb, and fire are examples of light **sources**. They emit light waves that travel through the spectrum. Some of the waves go directly into your eye, but many of them **reflect**, or bounce, off things first. Your eyes sense how these waves bounce around in the space that surrounds you. Reflecting light waves give the world shape and color.

Each color is a different wave in the spectrum. When all the waves of color are combined, they create white light. **Prisms** separate the different waves of color that are found in white light. A prism creates a rainbow, which is white light divided into all the different colors it contains.

The objects that surround you **absorb** some light waves and reflect others. This is how you see color. For example, if you see a friend wearing a red shirt, that shirt is reflecting only red light waves. The shirt is absorbing all the other waves of color, so you see only red. White objects reflect every color, and black objects absorb every color.

On Earth, it's hard to see that light needs time to move around. A lightning strike several miles away still reaches your eye in an instant. Light from the sun, though, has to cross about 93 million miles of space to reach Earth. Even at 186,000 miles per second, sunlight takes about eight minutes to get here. Proxima Centauri, the next closest star after the sun, is 4.22 **light-years** away. Its light traveled for more than four years to reach your eye.

Circle the letter of the best answer to each question below.

1. All light

    a. is ultraviolet light.

    b. moves in waves.

    c. bounces off the spectrum.

    d. comes from space.

2. A prism shows that

    a. light is a wave.

    b. radio waves are part of the spectrum.

    c. white light contains all colors.

    d. All of the above

3. The light from a light bulb

    a. travels at 186,000 miles per second.

    b. reflects off objects in the room.

    c. moves in waves.

    d. All of the above

Write your answers on the lines below.

4. Explain why a banana is yellow.

    _____

    _____

5. How are light, radio waves, and microwave ovens related?

    _____

    _____

What's Next?

Like any color, the color of the sky depends on light waves. See if you can find out why the sky is blue during the day and orange or pink when the sun is setting.

Review

Circle the letter of the best answer to each question below.

1. Which of the following statements is not true according to Newton's laws?

   a. If you kick a moving ball, it will keep moving in the same direction at the same speed.

   b. It takes more force for an adult to do a pull-up than a child.

   c. The reason you don't fall through the floor is that the floor is pushing back against you.

   d. A toy car in motion will stop rolling if a box is placed in front of it.

2. A grape that is left out in the sun will shrivel up and become a tiny raisin. The grape became smaller because many of its atoms and molecules

   a. were destroyed.

   b. became smaller.

   c. floated away as gases.

   d. All of the above

3. You can't see molecules moving in water because

   a. they move too slowly.

   b. they move too quickly.

   c. they are transparent.

   d. they are too small.

4. The yellowish-orange color of a flame is caused by

   a. glowing dust particles.

   b. fire.

   c. burnt gases.

   d. oxygen.

Write your answers on the lines below.

5. Fire is a _____ reaction.

6. _____ and _____ are two examples of fuels for fire.

7. Electricity will flow through a(n) _____ circuit, but not through a(n) _____ circuit.

8. What are three states of matter? _____ _____ _____

9. Give one example of something that has changed from one state of matter to another.

_____

10. How did Mr. Harris's experiment with food coloring and water prove that molecules are always in motion?

_____

_____

11. In the buoyancy experiment, why did the jar float in the salt water but not in the unsalted water?

_____

_____

12. Why is it difficult to swim in the very salty Dead Sea?

_____

13. Which color or colors does a blue box absorb? Which color or colors does it reflect?

_____

_____

Fill in the blanks in the sentences below with words from the box.

| physical | fuel | accelerated | displace | reflect | current | force | chemical |

14. Something that causes an object to begin moving is a _____ .

15. A car that has begun moving faster has _____ .

16. An object will _____, or push aside, its own weight in water.

17. When a substance changes states, it has gone through a _____ change.

18. Light waves _____ off the things around you to give the world shape and color.

19. When a substance's molecules gain or lose atoms, a _____ change has taken place.

20. Without _____, heat, and oxygen, a fire can't burn.

21. A battery produces an electrical _____ when it is part of a circuit.

Lesson 3.1   A Name for Every Living Thing

botanist: a scientist who studies plants

genus: a group of plants or animals that are related to each other; usually includes several species

species: a category of living things of the same kind

classify: to sort into groups or classes

People around the world use the same scientific names for organisms, no matter what language they speak. A cat is known as *Felis catus* in Russia, Japan, and Brazil.

"What's in a name? That which we call a rose by any other name would smell as sweet." —William Shakespeare, playwright and poet

Here is how Linnaeus classified human beings:
Kingdom—Animal
Phylum—Chordates
Class—Mammals
Order—Primates
Family—Hominidae
Genus—*Homo*
Species—*sapiens*

Scientists believe there are over ten million species on Earth. So far, they have discovered about 1.7 million.

What kind of groups do scientists use to talk about plants and animals?

People have been naming things in the natural world for thousands of years. The names gave them a way to talk about the world around them. How else would they tell someone that a plant was good for curing an illness or let people know when a poisonous spider was discovered? If everyone used the same names, they could communicate with each other.

Scientists also wanted to be able to organize the information they had about the natural world. The best way they knew to do this was to give Latin names to plants, animals, and other organisms. The names they used were often very long, though. For example, the tomato was known as *Solanum caule inermi herbaceo, foliis pinnatis incisis*. These Latin names were difficult to remember. They were tough to say, too.

It was also hard to keep track of all the plants that were being found as Europeans explored the New World. It was confusing when people who spoke different languages called the same organism by different names.

Carolus Linnaeus changed all that in the mid-1700s. Linnaeus was a **botanist** and a medical doctor. He was very interested in plants. He grew many types himself. He also traveled a lot to learn about new plants. Because Linnaeus spent so much time working with plants, he wanted to have an easier way to talk about them. He decided to use a two-part name. Linnaeus's method caught on. People liked how easy it was to use, and it replaced the old system.

Linnaeus's two-part name was made up of a **genus** and **species**. This system is still in use today. The genus always comes first. It is capitalized and is a more general name. The species, which is not capitalized, is more specific. It might describe the plant or animal, tell where it is found, or give the name of the person who discovered it. The genus *Canis* includes wolves, dogs, and coyotes. *Canis latrans* is used to describe coyotes. *Canis lupus* is a wolf.

Today, seven categories help scientists **classify** living things. The categories go in order from general to specific: kingdom, phylum, class, order, family, genus, and species. They help people understand the way living things are similar to and different from one another.

Read each sentence below. Underline the correct answer from the two choices you are given.

1. In the classification system, a kingdom is more (general, specific) than an order.

2. Scientific names are (the same, different) all around the world.

3. The scientific name for (dogs, human beings) is *Homo sapiens*.

4. A flea, a tree, a rabbit, and a mushroom are all examples of (genuses, organisms).

5. A botanist is a scientist who studies (plants, animal behavior).

Write your answers on the lines below.

6. Why did Linnaeus start using a different method of classification?

_____

7. Why do scientists classify living things?

_____

_____

8. The scientific name for the tiger is *Panthera tigris*. To what genus does the tiger belong?

_____ What species is it? _____

9. *Panthera pardus* is the scientific name for the leopard. How are the leopard and tiger related?

_____

10. Can two different animals have the exact same scientific name? Explain why or why not.

_____

_____

What's Next?

Choose any animal and find out how scientists classify it. Find the information to fill each of the categories. If you have trouble remembering what they are, think of a device to help you. The first letter of each word can stand for something in a silly saying, like "**K**atie **p**repares **c**old **o**lives **f**or **G**ary's **s**upper."

Ready to Eat

omnivores: animals that eat both plants and other animals

carnivores: animals that eat only meat

nutrients: chemicals that provide what is needed for growth and development

herbivores: animals that eat only plant materials

Words that end in **vore** describe what different kinds of animals eat. They come from the Latin word *vorare*, which means "to devour." Find an example of each of the animals listed below.

- **Insectivores** are carnivores that eat mostly insects.
- **Sanguinivores** are animals that drink blood.
- **Mucivores** are insects that eat plant juices.
- **Piscivores** are animals that eat mostly fish.
- **Frugivores** are animals that eat mostly fruit.

Plants can be carnivores, too. Some eat insects, but others can even trap small animals.

Not all carnivores kill the animals they eat. Scavengers, like vultures, feed on animals that are already dead.

What kind of eater are you? What about your dog or your cat?

What do you eat for dinner? For many people, some type of meat, vegetable, and grain make up the evening meal. That's because most human beings are **omnivores**. Omnivores have bodies that are suited to eating animals and plants. You've probably noticed that you have several different kinds of teeth. Some are sharp and pointy. They are used for biting and tearing meat. Others are flat and wide. These teeth are better for grinding, which is useful for eating fruits and vegetables. Raccoons, bears, foxes, rats, and pigs are other examples of omnivores.

Carnivores are animals that live almost completely by eating other animals. Carnivores have teeth and claws that help them hunt and eat their prey. Their jaws move mainly up and down, which is the motion they need for tearing and chewing large pieces of meat. Their stomach juices contain strong acids that break down the chunks of meat. The acids also kill bacteria in the raw meat to keep the carnivore from getting sick.

Lions, polar bears, and wolves are common examples of carnivores. Seals, walruses, snakes, vultures, ferrets, and spiders are carnivores, too. Even though they eat only meat, carnivores actually need the **nutrients** found in plants. Their teeth and digestive systems are not suited for eating plant materials, though. When carnivores eat **herbivores**, or plant-eating animals, they get the nutrition they need.

The small intestine of an herbivore is very long—about 10 to 12 times the length of the animal's body. This gives herbivores plenty of space to digest tough plant materials. The stomachs of cows and sheep have four chambers, or sections, to help them digest hay and grasses.

Herbivores also have special teeth that are useful for their diet of plants. The front teeth of rodents, like beavers, grow constantly and are shaped like tiny chisels. This lets them gnaw on tough plant material, like tree bark. Deer, grasshoppers, rabbits, and elephants are all examples of herbivores.

Circle the letter of the best answer to the question below.

1. The leopard, crocodile, cheetah, and sea lion are examples of which type of animal?

   a. herbivore

   b. carnivore

   c. omnivore

   d. Both a and b

Write **true** or **false** next to each statement below.

2. _____ The jaws of carnivores move easily from side to side.

3. _____ An omnivore might eat both fish and berries.

4. _____ Stomach acids in carnivores kill the bacteria found in raw meat.

5. _____ Herbivores have very short small intestines.

Write your answers on the lines below.

6. How do carnivores get the nutrients found in plants? Explain.

   _____

7. Some animals have a diet that depends on the season. When it is warm outside, they may eat a lot of nuts, berries, and grasses. When snow covers the ground, they rely on other animals as a source of food. What type of eater is this animal?

   _____

   _____

8. Explain two ways that the bodies of carnivores and herbivores are different.

   _____

   _____

   _____

Unifying Concepts and Processes

What are two reasons why scientists might divide animals into groups, like carnivores, herbivores, and omnivores?

_____

_____

Microscopic Marvels

abundant: existing in great numbers

marine: of the sea

estimated: judged by experience or observation, but not actually measured; guessed

In some places, there are so many phytoplankton that they color huge areas of the sea. Red tides are an example of this happening. A certain kind of phytoplankton turns red when it dies, making the sea look red. Red tides can be dangerous. The water becomes poisonous because it has such a strong concentration of this one phytoplankton.

The Red Sea gets its name from the red tides that occur there.

The blue whale—the largest animal on Earth—survives on tiny plankton. Although its mouth could fit dozens of people, its throat is much smaller. It can't swallow anything wider than a couple of feet.

Do you know why plankton are important to every animal on Earth?

Most plankton are so tiny, they can't be seen with the naked eye. Yet they are one of Earth's most **abundant** and important organisms. Plankton aren't spread evenly through Earth's oceans, seas, and lakes. They are too small to swim against the currents and tides. Instead, plankton are concentrated into huge groups that drift wherever the water takes them.

There are two kinds of plankton—phytoplankton and zooplankton. Phytoplankton are plants. They are the lowest level of the **marine** food chain. This means all marine animals depend on phytoplankton.

Although single phytoplankton are too small to see, they can be seen in large groups. Because they're plants, phytoplankton contain chlorophyll—the chemical that helps plants produce their own food and makes them green. A green patch of algae floating on the water's surface is actually millions of phytoplankton clumped together.

Phytoplankton and zooplankton live together in the water. Zooplankton are tiny marine animals. They range in size from microscopic to a few inches long. They eat phytoplankton, so they are the second step in the marine food chain. Zooplankton are eaten by larger marine animals.

Although you might imagine fish swimming throughout the ocean, many areas don't have any fish at all. On land, plants are at the bottom of the food chain. Few animals live in the deserts or Antarctica because there are few, if any, plants. The ocean isn't any different. You find fish and other marine animals wherever plankton are concentrated.

Phytoplankton don't just play an important role in the marine food chain. Every animal on Earth depends on them for another reason. Like all plants, phytoplankton use carbon dioxide to make food. Then, they emit oxygen as a waste product. It's **estimated** that phytoplankton produce nearly three-quarters of Earth's oxygen.

Pollution and Earth's warming climate are creating problems for plankton. These tiny plants and animals thrive in cool ocean water. When the water's temperature rises by even just one or two degrees, the plankton have a difficult time surviving. Polluting chemicals can also kill plankton. Without plankton, larger marine life doesn't have anything to eat. These microscopic marvels are definitely worth protecting.

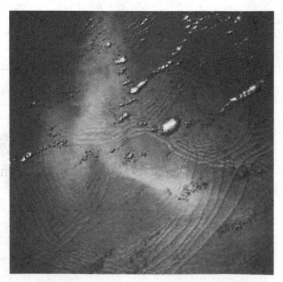

Circle the letter of the best answer to each question below.

1. Plankton are

   a. plants.

   b. animals.

   c. Both a and b

   d. None of the above

2. Plankton are

   a. spread evenly throughout the oceans.

   b. concentrated in large groups.

   c. eaten by zooplankton

   d. at the top of the ocean's food chain.

Write **true** or **false** next to each statement below.

3. _____ Zooplankton are at the bottom of the marine food chain.

4. _____ Phytoplankton need sunlight to make food.

5. _____ Some plankton can be seen without a microscope.

6. _____ Phytoplankton produce at least three-quarters of Earth's carbon dioxide.

Write your answers on the lines below.

7. Explain why every marine animal depends on phytoplankton.

   _____

8. Explain why the author says that some parts of the ocean are like a desert.

   _____

   _____

Unifying Concepts and Processes

Scientific terms come from Latin and Greek words. The word *plankton* comes from the Greek word *planktos*, which means "drifter." The Greek word *phyton* means "plant," and *zoon* means "animal." What do you think a bacterioplankton is?

_____

A Mysterious Mammal

characteristics: qualities or appearances that make one thing different from another

secrete: to produce or give off a substance

receptors: cells or groups of cells that receive information

burrow: a hole made by an animal for shelter or protection

A platypus's bill might look somewhat like a duck's bill, but they are made of different materials. A duck's bill is very hard. A platypus's bill is made of soft bone, called *cartilage*. It's flexible, like your nose or ears, which are also made of cartilage.

The platypus is often called a *living fossil*. Although it is classified as a mammal, it has characteristics of both mammals and reptiles. There are no animals closely related to it living today, but the fossil of an ancient relative of the platypus was found that is more than 100 million years old.

What is poisonous, warm-blooded, lays eggs, and has a bill like a duck?

Birds lay eggs. Reptiles, amphibians, and insects lay eggs, too. But did you ever hear of a mammal laying eggs? Welcome to the world of the platypus. It's one of only a few egg-laying mammals on Earth—which is just one of the strange facts about this unique creature.

A platypus has a wide bill on the front of its face, although the platypus isn't related to birds at all. Its body is similar to an otter's or a beaver's body. It has a thick coat of fur, webbed feet, and a wide, flat tail. These **characteristics** make platypuses great swimmers. Male platypuses are poisonous. They have spikes on the backs of their feet that **secrete** a poison.

Platypuses are found only in eastern Australia and on the island of Tasmania. When the first Europeans saw platypuses in the late 1700s, they couldn't believe the animal was real. A stuffed specimen was sent back to England, and a scientist began cutting into it looking for stitches. He was sure someone had sewn together parts from several different animals.

Platypuses make their homes near streams and rivers. They spend a large part of each day underwater. Usually, a platypus will spend only a few minutes underwater searching for food. Sometimes, though, platypuses will rest at the bottom of a river for a much longer time. Their heart rates drop to only ten beats per minute so they don't use too much oxygen.

Platypuses usually hunt for their food at night. They can't see much in the dark water. Instead, they use special **receptors** in their bills to locate prey. A platypus's prey will send tiny amounts of electricity into the water whenever its muscles move. The platypus uses its receptors to sense this electricity and find its prey. The platypus is a carnivore that eats shrimp, crayfish, worms, beetles, and other large insects.

In late winter or spring, the female platypus lays one to three eggs. They're tiny—less than one inch in diameter—and stick to the fur of her belly. She curls up in a **burrow** for nearly two weeks, protecting the eggs and keeping them warm. When the babies hatch, they are about the size of a jellybean. Four months later, they've grown to nearly adult size and are ready to leave the burrow.

Circle the letter of the best answer to each question below.

1. The platypus is a

   a. mammal.

   b. reptile.

   c. amphibian.

   d. All of the above

2. The receptors in a platypus's bill sense

   a. light.

   b. movement.

   c. electricity.

   d. odors.

Write your answers on the lines below.

3. How is a platypus's bill different from a duck's bill?

   _____

   _____

4. Explain why a platypus's heart rate must slow down so it can stay underwater for long periods of time.

   _____

   _____

Unifying Concepts and Processes

The theory of evolution states that animals evolve, or change, over time. Millions of years ago, reptiles were the largest animals on Earth. They were at the top of the food chain. Today, mammals are the largest animals. They have replaced reptiles at the top of the food chain. Why do you think scientists believe the platypus is an important clue in the history of evolution?

   _____

   _____

   _____

Creatures of the Night

nocturnal: active during the night

diurnal: active during the day

predator: an animal that hunts other animals

adapting: adjusting to fit a new situation

echolocation: a way of locating things using sound waves

Most ancient mammals were nocturnal. Dinosaurs were their greatest threat, and dinosaurs were active during the day. After the giant reptiles became extinct, there were fewer daytime threats for many mammals. They evolved over time, and many became diurnal.

Most sea turtles are diurnal, except when they are nesting. They bury their eggs in the sand under the cover of night. When the baby turtles hatch, they make the dangerous trip across the sand to the sea at night, too.

Owls, raccoons, badgers, skunks, hamsters, possums, moths, foxes, hedgehogs, and bats are common nocturnal animals.

Why do some animals become active after dark?

Have you ever heard the bang of a trashcan lid in the middle of the night? A visiting raccoon may have woken you up as it searched for a snack. That's because raccoons are **nocturnal** animals—they are active during the night and sleep during the day. Human beings, like many animals, are **diurnal**. They are awake during the day and sleep when it's dark outside.

What do animals do when it is dark outside? It seems like nighttime hunting would be more difficult. That's actually part of the reason why many small animals are nocturnal. If they didn't remain hidden for most of the day, they might be caught and eaten by a **predator**. Some animals have a better chance of surviving if they are active under the cover of night.

Over time, some predators have become nocturnal, too. Owls feed on small animals, like mice. By **adapting** their sleeping habits, owls can hunt nocturnal creatures.

Many desert animals are active at night for a very different reason. During the day, the sun is scorching hot. Temperatures are often above 100°F. Animals burrow under a rock or into the sand where it's cooler and wait until the sun sets to come out.

Nocturnal animals tend to have excellent hearing and a sharp sense of smell. Their eyes are also well suited for seeing at night. Owls and bush babies, for example, have very large eyes. Many tiny rods in the backs of their eyes collect more light. Have you ever noticed how a cat's eyes look like they are glowing when light is shined at them in the dark? This is because a special part of their eyes acts like a mirror and reflects the light.

Not all nocturnal animals have good night vision. Bats rely on **echolocation**, not sight, to find insects in the dark. They send out very high-pitched sounds, most too high for the human ear to hear. When the sound hits an object, like a mosquito, it bounces back. The bat can tell where the insect is, how big it is, and whether it's moving.

Ask an adult to take a nighttime walk with you. The human world quiets down after dark, but many in the animal world are just awakening. Keep your eyes and ears open, and there will be plenty to observe.

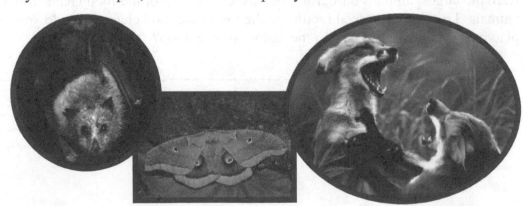

Circle the letter of the best answer to each question below.

1. Many desert animals are nocturnal because

   a. they cannot sleep at night.

   b. there are many predators out at night.

   c. they try to avoid the extreme heat of the day.

   d. None of the above

2. An animal that has extra rods in the backs of its eyes will

   a. have poor night vision.

   b. have better night vision.

   c. use echolocation.

   d. not be able to see at all.

Write your answers on the lines below.

3. How are nocturnal and diurnal animals different?

   _____

   _____

4. In your own words, explain how echolocation works. Why does it allow bats to be nocturnal creatures?

   _____

   _____

5. How have owls adapted their behavior? Why did they do this?

   _____

   _____

6. Explain why you think sea turtles nest at night and why the newly-hatched babies make their way to the sea at night.

   _____

   _____

Swamp Life

What kind of tree keeps its roots above ground?

If you were to water a household plant with salt water, it wouldn't live very long. Even so, some very odd plants and trees have found a way to live in a salty environment. It's lucky that they do, too, because they create a home for hundreds of other species.

Mangrove swamps are distinctive **ecosystems** located in warm parts of the world. They are found in sheltered coastal areas, like bays and lagoons. Mangroves swamps are muddy and filled with salty water. Even though most plants wouldn't be able to live there, mangrove trees and shrubs do quite well. They have large root systems that look like stilts or long fingers. Because most of the tree's roots are so far above ground, the body of the tree doesn't get covered in salt water at high tide. A thick tangle of roots also lie below the soil and help anchor the tree in place.

The roots of the mangroves act as a **filter**. They keep **sediment** from the land from flowing into the ocean. They also protect the land. They keep it from **eroding** too quickly. During large storms, mangrove swamps can keep land near the water from flooding. They also filter out pollution.

One of the most important roles of the mangrove swamp is to provide a **habitat** for animals. The swamps are a perfect home for many species—from tiny bacteria to huge manatees. The gnarly roots of the mangroves provide protection for small creatures. They even act as a sort of nursery for some types of marine wildlife. The young grow up under the shelter of the mangrove trees before they head out to the more dangerous seas.

The moist, muddy mangroves are home to at least two dozen species of reptiles and amphibians. Some of the saltwater crocodiles that live there measure more than 20 feet in length. More than 200 species of fish also live in the swamps. Water birds, like storks and egrets, get plenty of tasty meals there. They have no trouble finding fish, frogs, and insects to eat. Even mammals, like raccoons, otters, bats, bears, minks, and deer, live in and around mangrove swamps.

Circle the letter of the best answer to each question below.

1. Mangrove trees are different than other types of trees because
   a. they can live in a saltwater environment.
   b. they need air and sunlight to live.
   c. most of their roots are above ground.
   d. Both a and c

2. Which of the following statements is not true?
   a. Mangrove swamps act as a filter.
   b. Most mangrove swamps are located in cold, northern areas of the country.
   c. The swamps need the help of human beings to survive.
   d. Hundreds of species of animals make their homes in mangrove swamps.

Write your answers on the lines below.

3. Why is a mangrove swamp an ecosystem?

   _____

4. What are two ways that the tangled roots of a mangrove swamp protect nearby land?

   _____

   _____

5. Why do the mangrove swamps make a good nursery for young marine animals?

   _____

   _____

6. Why are mangrove trees so strange looking? How does the way they look help them live in their habitat?

   _____

   _____

   _____

What's Next?

Learn more about the creatures that live in mangrove swamps. What makes the swamps a perfect home for them? How are the animals in U.S. mangrove swamps different from those in Australia or Africa?

Underground Farmers

decompose: to break down into smaller parts

castings: the waste product of worms

Worms have five pairs of hearts. They have no lungs, so they breathe through their skin.

If a small piece of a worm is cut off, it can grow back.

Even though worms don't have eyes, their bodies are sensitive to light. They can't see, but they can tell the difference between light and dark.

You've probably noticed that a worm doesn't have legs. It moves by squeezing together the circular muscles that run along the length of its body.

"It may be doubted whether there are many other animals in the world which have played so important a part in the history of the world [as earthworms]."
—Charles Darwin, naturalist

Why are worms such a valuable part of life on this planet?

Worms aren't very popular creatures. Some people even find them to be slimy and gross. Maybe if more people knew how important worms are to life on Earth, they'd have a different opinion.

It might not sound like a tasty diet to you, but worms eat soil, dead animals, and plant materials, like leaves. They help **decompose**, or break, all these things down. In the course of a day, worms eat more than their own body weight. Their waste, or **castings**, is sometimes called *black gold* because it is so rich in nutrients that plants need. As they eat, worms burrow and tunnel. These tunnels are also good for plants. They are like little vents that allow more air and water to flow through the soil.

How to Make a Wormery

Materials: a large glass jar, soil, sand, dead leaves, some grass clippings, a piece of black cloth, 3 or 4 earthworms, a spray bottle filled with water

- Spray the soil with water so that it is slightly damp, but not wet. Put some soil in the jar and then add a smaller layer of sand. Add another layer of each and then place the worms in the jar. Then, keep alternating layers until the jar is about three-quarters full.

- Now, place the grass clippings and leaves on the top layer of soil or sand. Cover the jar with the black cloth, and put it someplace cool. Remember, worms are used to living underground.

- After a few days, lift the cloth from the jar and see what has happened. You'll probably notice that the worms have started digging tunnels. They may have already begun to mix the sand and soil together. They might also have dragged some of the leaves and grass below the surface.

- If you keep the soil moist, you can keep the worms for a week or two so that you can observe them at work. After that time, you'll need to release them, unless you want to keep giving them new material to eat.

Circle the letter of the best answer to each question below.

1. Why are worm castings called *black gold*?

   a. Gold can also be used as a fertilizer for plants.

   b. They are found in the same place gold is.

   c. They cost the same amount per ounce as gold does.

   d. They make an excellent fertilizer for plants.

2. Why would a gardener be happy to find worms in his or her garden?

   a. They are a sign that the soil is healthy.

   b. They keep garden pests away.

   c. They attract other helpful creatures to the garden.

   d. Both b and c

3. If you don't put a black cloth over the wormery, the worms will stay hidden toward the center of the jar and you won't be able to see them. Why do you think this is?

   a. They will think it is nighttime.

   b. They are used to living underground and are sensitive to light.

   c. The bright light will hurt their eyes.

   d. The worms will be too scared to come out where they can be seen.

Write your answers on the lines below.

4. What are two good things that earthworms do for the soil?

   _____

   _____

5. What do the worms in the wormery eat?

   _____

Unifying Concepts and Processes

Worms are very important to all forms of life on this planet. Explain why this is.

   _____

   _____

Circle the letter of the best answer to each question below.

1. The scientific name for the cucumber is *Cucumis sativus*. *Cucumis* is the plant's

   a. genus.

   b. species.

   c. family.

   d. kingdom.

2. Plankton are an important part of Earth's ecosystem because

   a. they are at the top of the marine food chain.

   b. they produce a huge percentage of Earth's oxygen.

   c. they kill bacteria in the ocean.

   d. Both a and b

3. How have platypuses evolved so that they can hunt underwater at night?

   a. They have eyes that can see in the dark.

   b. They have special receptors in their bills that sense electricity.

   c. They have special receptors in their ears that sense movement.

   d. They have a very sharp sense of smell underwater.

4. Mangroves are an important part of their coastal ecosystems because

   a. their roots filter out sediment and pollution from the water.

   b. their roots keep land from eroding away.

   c. they provide habitats for many different kinds of animals.

   d. All of the above

Write your answers on the lines below.

5. Why is it important for scientists to use the same names for plants and animals when they talk to other scientists?

   _____

6. _____ is a more specific category than *genus*.

7. Human beings have both sharp, pointy teeth and flat, wide teeth because human beings

   are _____.

8. What is the difference between phytoplankton and zooplankton?

_____

9. Explain why carnivores need strong acids in their stomachs.

_____

_____

10. What are two things that are threatening the plankton in Earth's oceans?

_____   _____

11. What makes the platypus different from other mammals?

_____

12. How do bats use echolocation to hunt at night?

_____

_____

13. Why are some animals nocturnal? Give at least two reasons.

_____

_____

14. Explain why earthworms are a sign of healthy soil.

_____

Draw a line from the word in column one to its definition in column two.

15. decompose   **a.** sort into groups

16. characteristics   **b.** existing in great numbers

17. habitat   **c.** animals that eat only plants

18. herbivores   **d.** to break down into smaller parts

19. adapting   **e.** qualities that make things different from each other

20. classify   **f.** adjusting to fit a new situation

21. abundant   **g.** the natural place where a plant or animal lives

NAME _____

Circle the letter of the best answer to each question below.

1. When water evaporates,

   a. it is changing states.

   b. its molecules are disappearing.

   c. it is melting.

   d. Both b and c

2. Andy put a rubber duck in a bucket of water, and it floated. The duck weighs three ounces, so what is the weight of the water that was displaced?

   a. 2 ounces

   b. 3 ounces

   c. 6 ounces

   d. Not enough information is given

Write your answers on the lines below.

Julio and Miranda want to find out how light affects eyes. They walked from a dark room into bright sunlight. Miranda watched Julio's pupils get smaller. When they walked back into the darker room, his pupils got much larger. When they turned on a nightlight, Julio's pupils barely changed at all.

3. What is the variable in this experiment? _____

4. What hypothesis do you think Julio and Miranda were testing?

   _____

5. What conclusion could Julio and Miranda draw?

   _____

6. Did Julio and Miranda use more than one method of investigation? Explain.

   _____

   _____

7. Name two roles that mangrove trees play in their ecosystem.

   _____

8. Describe what conditions a wormery should have.

   _____

9. What are the three things every fire needs? _____ _____ _____

10. Why did Linnaeus invent a new way to classify living things?

_____

11. Explain why the teeth of herbivores and carnivores are different.

_____

12. Why do all marine animals depend on phytoplankton?

_____

13. Place a check mark next to each system listed below.

_____ hammer   _____ squirrel   _____ dishwasher   _____ bowl   _____ a rock

14. You are in a boat on the water. You push against the dock, and the boat moves away in the opposite direction. Why?

_____

15. Explain the difference between closed and open circuits.

_____

Underline the correct answer from the two choices you are given.

16. The more (atoms, volume) something has the more mass it will have.

17. Steam is an example of water that has gone through a (chemical, physical) change.

18. When you put a battery into a device, it becomes part of a (current, circuit).

19. Light waves and radio waves are part of the (spectrum, air).

20. A predator is not a(n) (herbivore, carnivore).

21. Like all plants, phytoplankton emit (carbon dioxide, oxygen).

22. To escape the heat of the day, many desert animals are (nocturnal, diurnal.)

Write **true** or **false** next to each statement below.

23. _____ Newton's laws of motion tell you that it's easier to move a book than a couch.

24. _____ Atoms and molecules will stop moving in frozen substances.

25. _____ Flames are always orange or yellow in color.

26. _____ Objects that are black reflect every color of light.

Lesson 4.1   Nature's Ice Cubes

glaciers: large bodies of ice that move slowly through valleys or spread across the land

In 1912, an oceanliner called *Titanic* hit an iceberg and sank. The dangers icebergs pose to ships was brought to the attention of the world. In 1914, the International Ice Patrol was formed to track icebergs. It still performs this job today.

A large iceberg has a lot of freshwater frozen in it. Some scientists have suggested using icebergs as a water source. Icebergs would be towed to places that don't have much freshwater, where they would be melted.

Where do icebergs come from?

Like floating white mountains, icebergs drift through the seas near Earth's poles. Most icebergs are found in the Arctic Ocean or the waters surrounding Antarctica. They are huge pieces of freshwater ice floating in the ocean's salty water. Wind, weather, and sunlight slowly wear them away until nothing is left.

Land at or near Earth's poles is under thick layers of ice all year round. For example, the Ross Ice Shelf in Antarctica is hundreds of feet thick. Icebergs are created where **glaciers** and ice sheets meet the ocean. The ice sheets of Greenland and Antarctica produce most of Earth's icebergs. Giant chunks of ice break off and drop into the sea. This process is called *calving*. After an iceberg has calved, wind and waves push it away from the shore.

The frozen water in glaciers and ice sheets is freshwater. Icebergs don't sink because freshwater ice is less dense than salt water. Less than one-fifth of an iceberg's volume stays above the water's surface, though. The rest of it hides below the waves.

Icebergs can be divided into categories based on their shapes. Tabular icebergs have flat sides and flat tops. Their flat, horizontal shape means that they don't roll over. Rounded icebergs tumble and turn upside-down as they float along. Irregular icebergs have peaks and slopes. They look more like jagged mountains, or even strange castles.

Icebergs that have been at sea for a long time show signs of wear. Wind, waves, and weather carve caves and tunnels into the ice.

Ice chunks of all sizes litter the Arctic and Antarctic waters, but icebergs are pieces of ice at least 16 feet in diameter. There is no limit to how large they can get. In 2000, an iceberg the size of Jamaica calved off the Ross Ice Shelf.

Most icebergs survive for about four years before breaking up and melting away. Big icebergs can last for decades, though. For nearly 30 years, a giant iceberg in the northern Atlantic Ocean was used as a research station. Scientists built a power station, huts, and a landing strip on it. Eventually, it drifted into warmer water and broke apart just like any other iceberg.

Circle the letter of the best answer to each question below.

1. Icebergs float because

   a. they weigh less than salt water.

   b. they are smaller than the ocean.

   c. they are less dense than salt water.

   d. All of the above

2. Icebergs are formed

   a. when ocean water freezes.

   b. only during winter.

   c. by wind blowing across ocean waves.

   d. when chunks of ice break off ice sheets or glaciers.

Write **true** of **false** next to each statement below.

3. _____ Icebergs are never more than 16 miles in diameter.

4. _____ Most icebergs are found in the Arctic or Antarctica.

5. _____ All icebergs are freshwater ice.

6. _____ Only one-fifth of an iceberg's volume stays below water.

Write your answers on the lines below.

7. What is calving?

   _____

8. Icebergs float in very cold water, but they don't last forever. Why?

   _____

   _____

9. Which shape do you think the iceberg was that the scientists built their research station on? Why?

   _____

   _____

Strange but Beautiful

stalagmites: cave formations made of calcium carbonate that form on the floor of a cave

stalactites: cave formations made of calcium carbonate that hang from the ceiling of a cave

evaporates: changes from a liquid into a gas

column: the cave formation of calcium carbonate that reaches from the cave floor to its ceiling

It can take thousands of years for stalagmites and stalactites to form. They are fragile, so if you ever have a chance to see some, be sure not to touch them.

It's easy to remember the difference between the two. *Stalagmites* is spelled with a **g**, and stalagmites begin on the **g**round. *Stalactites* is spelled with a **c**, and stalactites are found on the **c**eiling of a cave.

Cavers, or people who explore caves, sometimes call the formations they see *pretties* or *cave decorations*.

What are cave formations, and how do they form?

Enter an underground cave, and you may think you're on a different planet. Icicle-shaped masses drip from above and seem to sprout from the ground. What are these strange things? They are cave formations, called **stalagmites** and **stalactites**.

Groundwater—water within Earth—moves through soil and rocks and picks up minerals. Many of the caves where formations are found are made of limestone, which is high in calcium. Over time, water seeps very slowly through the roof of a cave. Little droplets cling to the ceiling. The water in the droplets **evaporates**, or turns to gas, leaving behind deposits of calcium. Over time, more water continues to seep into the cave. This steady dripping forms stalactites.

Some water also drips onto the floor of the cave. When this happens in the same spot over and over, the calcium deposits build up and form stalagmites. When a stalagmite and a stalactite meet, a **column** is created. A column can also form if a stalactite grows so long that it reaches the floor of the cave.

Make Your Own Stalactites

You can make your own stalactites at home. All you need are two jars, some Epsom salts or baking soda, cotton string, a baking sheet, and a couple of metal washers or other weights.

- Fill both jars with warm water. Mix in as much baking soda or Epsom salts as will dissolve.

- Cut a piece of string that measures about one and a half feet long. Tie one washer to each end of the string, and place the washers in the jars. Then, place the jars about a foot away from one another on the baking sheet.

- Leave the jars alone for a few days. When you check them again, you'll notice that stalactites have begun to form on the string. The water will be drawn up the string, and as it slowly drips down, it will leave behind the minerals in the baking soda or Epsom salts. This is very similar to the way real cave formations are created underground.

Circle the letter of the best answer to each question below.

1. A column forms when

   a. a stalagmite and stalactite grow together.

   b. a stalactite grows so long it reaches the floor of the cave.

   c. part of a stalactite breaks off and begins growing again from the cave floor.

   d. Both a and b

2. Stalagmites and stalactites are types of

   a. minerals.

   b. cave formations.

   c. groundwater.

   d. limestone.

Choose the word from the box that best completes each sentence.

groundwater	calcium	ground	ceiling

3. In the experiment, the string is like the _____ of the cave.

4. The water in the jars is like the _____ that seeps into the cave from above.

5. Stalagmites are formed from the buildup of calcium on the _____ in a cave.

6. The water that drips into a cave contains _____ .

Write your answers on the lines below.

7. In your own words, explain how a stalactite forms.

   _____

   _____

8. Why do you think baking soda or Epsom salts work well in the experiment?

   _____

   _____

A Metal of Many Uses

aluminum: an abundant light, silvery metal

mined: dug for and taken from Earth

bauxite: a common soft mineral that is mined and converted to aluminum

recycling: changing something so that it can be used again

greenhouse gases: gases in Earth's atmosphere that trap heat and cause the planet to become warmer

In the 1800s, people were still trying to find a good way to separate aluminum from other substances. For a brief time, it was more valuable than gold or silver. When better methods of producing it were found, it fell in price.

An aluminum cap was placed at the top of the Washington Monument in 1884. It weighed 100 ounces. One ounce of aluminum was worth about twice what one of the workers on the monument earned in a day.

What's the world's most common metal, and where does it come from?

How many things made of metal can you see from where you are right now? The legs of a desk or chair, the hinges of a door, a soda can, and the rings of a spiral notebook are just a few things you might be able to spot. Even though metal is used in all sorts of places today, most people don't think much about where it comes from.

The most common metal in Earth's crust is **aluminum**. Aluminum has a lot of good qualities. It is both strong and lightweight. If you had a piece of aluminum and a piece of steel that were the same size, the aluminum would weigh only about one-third of the weight of the steel. This makes it perfect for all kinds of common uses. What could be a better material for airplanes? The lighter a plane is, the less fuel is needed to move it. A plane must be strong, though, and be able to face high winds, changes in temperature, and bad weather.

Aluminum also has a built-in protection. When it comes in contact with air, a thin layer forms on it. This keeps it from rusting. That's a good thing, because aluminum siding is often used on houses. Who'd want to live in a rusty house? Aluminum can also be made very thin and used for packaging. Aluminum foil protects food and keeps it tasting fresh. It doesn't leave behind any odor or affect the contents of the package.

One problem with this silvery metal is that it is never found alone, the way a metal like gold is. It is always combined with something else. Once it is **mined**, it needs to be separated from the other material. This can be difficult and expensive. That's why a mineral called **bauxite** is the most common source of aluminum. It is much easier to convert, or change, bauxite into aluminum. More than one hundred million tons of bauxite are mined each year.

There's not much chance that Earth's bauxite supply will run out anytime soon. That doesn't mean you should stop **recycling** your aluminum cans. Making new aluminum from old cans takes only about 5% of the energy needed to make aluminum in the first place. This also means that fewer **greenhouse gases**—gases that can be harmful to Earth—are released.

Circle the letter of the best answer to each question below.

1. Which of the following statements is true?

   a. Aluminum is a strong metal, but it rusts easily.

   b. Aluminum should not be used around food.

   c. Aluminum is much less dense than steel.

   d. Both b and c

2. What effect does air have on aluminum?

   a. It causes a protective layer to form.

   b. It causes the aluminum to rust.

   c. It makes the aluminum weaker.

   d. It makes aluminum harder to recycle.

Write your answers on the lines below.

3. What is one way in which aluminum and gold are similar? How are they different?

   _____

   _____

4. Name one of aluminum's good qualities and explain why that quality makes it a useful metal.

   _____

   _____

5. Is it better to make new things from recently mined aluminum or recycle aluminum products? Why?

   _____

   _____

Unifying Concepts and Processes

At one point in history, aluminum was a semiprecious metal and very valuable. Today, it is used in things that people often throw away. Why did this change take place?

   _____

   _____

Bottled Raindrops

currents: streams of air or liquid moving in a single direction

condenses: gas that changes to a liquid

compresses: uses pressure to reduce the space or volume of something

expands: increases in size, amount, or volume

Water collecting on the lid of a pot is an example of condensation. Steam is less dense than water because its molecules are spread farther apart. The lid of the pot is much cooler than the boiling water or the steam. When the rising steam hits the lid, it cools down quickly. The drop in temperature causes the water molecules to condense. The steam turns back into liquid water that clings to the lid.

How does moisture in the sky become a cloud?

Sammy Science asked the students at the Science Emporium, "What's inside a cloud?"

"Rain!" someone shouted.

"Yes, a cloud contains water," Sammy agreed, "but rain is the droplets that are too heavy to be in the cloud anymore. The droplets inside a cloud are smaller. They're light enough float on air **currents**."

Sammy explained that air always moves from areas of high pressure to areas of low pressure. As an example, he described air trapped in a balloon. "If you untie the balloon, the air rushes out because it moves from an area of high pressure to one of low pressure."

"In Earth's atmosphere," Sammy continued, "the pressure is lower than it is near the surface, so currents flow upward. They carry moisture with them. Molecules have more room to move, so the temperature drops. When moisture in the air cools, it **condenses**. In Earth's atmosphere, the droplets condense onto dust particles, and a cloud is created. Now, let's make our own cloud."

Sammy set a plastic pop bottle on the table. He poured about an inch of warm water into it, tightened the cap, and shook it up. "Now there are tiny droplets floating inside the bottle," he explained. Sammy squeezed the bottle ten times. Then, he held the final squeeze for ten seconds. Sammy placed the bottle in front of a black cloth, lit a match, and quickly blew it out. He uncapped the bottle and held the match so that smoke drifted inside. Then, he capped it tightly again.

He waited for the smoke to disappear and then began squeezing the bottle again. "Squeezing the bottle **compresses** the space," Sammy explained. "Molecules have less room to move, so the temperature rises. When I stop squeezing, the space **expands** and the molecules have more room. The temperature drops. A drop in temperature causes the moisture to condense."

Sammy set the bottle in front of the black cloth again. A thin cloud had appeared inside. Sammy unscrewed the lid, and a puff of white escaped into the air. "And that's how you make a cloud in a bottle," he concluded.

NAME _____

Circle the letter of the best answer to each question below.

1. As you go higher in Earth's atmosphere,

   a. the air temperature drops.

   b. the air pressure drops.

   c. Both a and b

   d. None of the above

2. Moisture in the air _____ around dust particles to form a cloud.

   a. compresses

   b. condenses

   c. currents

   d. drops

3. Air currents move

   a. from low temperatures to high temperatures.

   b. from areas of low pressure to areas of high pressure.

   c. from areas of high pressure to areas of low pressure.

   d. from areas with strong wind to areas of no wind.

Write your answers on the lines below.

4. What role did smoke play inside the bottle so that a cloud would form?

   _____

   _____

5. Explain why grass is wet with dew in the morning.

   _____

   _____

Unifying Concepts and Processes

Inside a cloud, water changes states from a gas to a liquid. Describe what happens when water changes
states again and becomes a solid inside the cloud.

   _____

The Ever-Changing Moon

orbit: the circular path of one body, like a satellite, around another

visible: able to be seen

waxing: growing larger

gibbous moon: a moon that is nearly full

waning: growing smaller

The same side of the moon always faces Earth. It's impossible to see the other side of the moon from anywhere on the planet.

The second full moon to happen in one month is called a *blue moon*. This occurs only about once every two-and-a-half years. That's why the phrase "once in a blue moon" is used when people are talking about something that happens very rarely.

Astronauts that walked on the moon left their footprints behind. Because there is no wind or weather on the moon, the footprints will be there for a very long time.

Do you know what the different phases of the moon are?

Have you ever wondered why the moon seems to be a different shape depending on when you look at it? The moon doesn't actually change shape, of course. One side of the moon is always lit by the sun. As the moon moves in an **orbit** around Earth, the amount of the lit side that we can see from Earth changes. That's why the moon appears to change shape.

A new moon occurs when the sun and moon are on the same side of Earth. The lit side is facing away from Earth. The moon seems to have disappeared because its shadowed side is facing Earth. As the **visible** amount of moon increases, the moon is said to be in its **waxing** phases. The waxing crescent occurs when just a little sliver of moon can be seen.

About a week after a new moon, the moon has moved one quarter of the way around Earth. Now, you can see half of the lit side and half of the shadowed side. This is called the *first-quarter moon*. Remember, the moon doesn't have any light source of its own. It seems to glow in the night sky because it is reflecting the light of the sun.

The first-quarter moon is followed by a waxing **gibbous moon**. A gibbous moon is nearly full. When the sun and the moon are on opposite sides of Earth, the entire lit side of the moon faces Earth. The moon appears to be "full."

After a full moon, the visible part of the moon starts to decrease. The moon is said to be in its **waning** phases. First, there is a waning gibbous moon. It is followed by a last-quarter moon, when once again you can see half of the lit side and half of the shadowed side of the moon. The last-quarter moon is followed by a waning crescent, another sliver moon. When the next new moon takes place, about 29.5 days later, the moon has completed one orbit around Earth. Now, the whole cycle will begin again.

On the next clear night, go outside and see if you can spot the moon. Can you tell what phase it is in? If you watch it for several days in row, you should be able to tell if it is waxing or waning.

New Moon — Waxing Moon — First Quarter — Waxing Gibbous — Full Moon — Waning Gibbous — Third Quarter — Waning Crescent

Circle the letter of the best answer to each question below.

1. During a full moon,

   a. the entire moon is lit by the sun.

   b. three-quarters of the moon is lit by the sun.

   c. the entire lit side of the moon is visible from Earth.

   d. the moon appears to be completely dark.

2. A blue moon

   a. is a moon that reflects the blue color of the sky.

   b. is the second full moon in a month.

   c. is the second new moon in a month.

   d. can be seen at the end of each lunar cycle.

Use the words in the box to complete the sentences below.

sun	cycle	orbit	gibbous

3. A _____ moon appears to be nearly full.

4. A new moon occurs when the _____ and the moon are on the same side of Earth.

5. There are eight phases of the moon in each _____ .

6. The moon takes about 29.5 days to complete its _____ around Earth.

Write your answers on the lines below.

7. What is the difference between a waxing gibbous moon and a waning gibbous moon?

   _____

8. Explain why the moon appears to change shape.

   _____

   _____

What's Next?

Since the moon moves in a predictable pattern, you can find out how it will look at any time. Do some research on NASA's Web site to see how the moon will look on any day between 1990 and 2019.

Lesson 4.6 Planetary Weather

extreme: existing to a very great degree

atmosphere: the mass of gases surrounding a planet

The outer, visible layer of Jupiter's atmosphere is filled with clouds of ammonia. Scientists think that a layer of water clouds might lie just below it. Lightning strikes can be seen flashing underneath the ammonia—a sign that water is there. These lightning strikes are a thousand times more powerful than the ones on Earth.

The four inner planets are called the *terrestrial planets.* Mercury, Venus, Earth, and Mars are made mostly of rock. The four outer planets are called *gas giants.* Jupiter, Saturn, Uranus, and Neptune are made mostly of gases.

What's Saturday's forecast on Neptune?

When it's chilly outside, you put on a jacket. If it starts to rain, you open an umbrella. But what do you wear when it's -300ºF? How do you protect yourself from a storm that's as big as Earth? The **extreme** weather on other planets is like nothing you've ever experienced.

Earth's **atmosphere** helps keep temperatures stable. They don't jump wildly from one extreme to another. Earth's temperatures keep water as a liquid most of the time, which is good for living things. Life can't exist where water is ice or steam all the time.

Mercury, the planet closest to the sun, has a very thin atmosphere. The side that faces the sun soars to 800ºF. The other side plunges to nearly -300ºF. With almost no atmosphere, the parts of Mercury that get heat from the sun freeze again as soon as they face out toward space. The heat just drifts away.

Venus's atmosphere, however, is thick and dense. Heavy clouds of carbon dioxide cover the entire planet and trap heat inside. Even though Venus is twice as far from the sun as Mercury, the planet stays near 800ºF all the time.

After Earth, Mars is the next farthest planet from the sun. The Martian atmosphere is thin, but it does hold some heat. In fact, summers on Mars are around 70ºF. Come winter, though, the temperature drops to -220ºF.

Temperature changes cause air to move through an atmosphere, so Martian winds can be fierce. They often reach 250 miles per hour. Winds tearing across the dusty Martian surface kick up huge dust storms that circle the entire planet. The surface of Venus, on the other hand, has almost no wind because the temperature hardly ever changes.

Jupiter—the largest planet in our solar system—is made mostly of hydrogen and helium. Jupiter's most famous feature is the Great Red Spot. This giant red area in the clouds of Jupiter's atmosphere is a storm larger than our entire planet.

Saturn is made mostly of hydrogen and helium. Saturn's winds push the gases around at more than 1,100 miles per hour, making it the windiest planet of our solar system.

Uranus and Neptune are called the *ice giants.* Temperatures never rise above -300ºF in the atmospheres of either planet. They are so far from the sun that they receive none of its heat.

Circle the letter of the best answer to each question below.

1. Venus is

   a. the planet closest to the sun.

   b. a gas giant.

   c. the planet that stays the warmest.

   d. Both b and c

2. Saturn is the windiest planet. This information tells you that

   a. the temperature on Saturn is always about the same.

   b. the temperatures on Saturn can vary greatly.

   c. the gases in its atmosphere are very light.

   d. the gases in its atmosphere aren't very dense.

3. Jupiter, Saturn, Uranus, and Neptune are

   a. terrestrial planets.

   b. ice giants.

   c. gas giants.

   d. All of the above

Write your answers on the lines below.

4. List two characteristics that Earth and Venus have in common.

   _____

   _____

5. Big temperature changes on Mars create very strong winds. Mercury has even bigger temperature changes, but no wind. Why?

   _____

6. Explain why Earth's temperatures make it the perfect place for life, and why life doesn't exist on the other planets.

   _____

   _____

The Hubble Space Telescope

astronomers:
scientists who study
outer space

interference: the act
of blocking or getting
in the way of
something

nebula: a gigantic
cloud of dust and gas;
where stars are born

galaxy: a group of
billions of stars; our
sun is part of the
Milky Way galaxy

black hole: an
invisible area in space
with extremely strong
gravity; may be
formed from dead
stars

The Hubble Space
Telescope is named
for Edwin Hubble, a
famous astronomer.
One of his important
discoveries was that
some stars in the
night sky are actually
entire galaxies.

In the fall of 2003, the
Hubble Space
Telescope focused its
lenses for 11 days on
a tiny part of the night
sky. This spot was as
big as a grain of sand
held an arm's length
away. In that one
speck of sky, Hubble
discovered 10,000
galaxies.

Why was putting a telescope in space such a great idea?

Hundreds of years ago, stars filled the night skies. After sunset, the only light on Earth's surface came from flickering candles or the glow of a fireplace. Then, the invention of electric lights lit up the night. Earth's surface was no longer quite so dark during the night hours, but neither was the night sky. The faintest stars disappeared from view. **Astronomers** found that all those lights made telescopes less useful.

In 1990, the Hubble Space Telescope was launched. Orbiting nearly 400 miles above Earth's surface, there is no **interference** from human-made lights. It has given us some of the most amazing views ever seen of space.

Hubble was launched just in time to see a rare event. In 1994, its cameras sent images to Earth showing a comet crashing through the thick clouds of Jupiter's atmosphere. Comets are large, frozen balls of dust, gas, and water. They usually orbit the sun. This comet had been captured by Jupiter's gravity, and for several years, had orbited the planet instead. Now, it was being pulled down to the planet's surface. This impact was the first observed impact of two space objects.

One of Hubble's most famous images shows the Eagle Nebula. A **nebula** is a gigantic cloud of dust and gas, and it's where stars are born. Gravity inside these clouds pulls together dust particles. After millions of years, these clumps of dust grow enormous, and they begin to form stars.

Many scientists think that every **galaxy** has a **black hole** at its center. The billions of stars that fill each galaxy slowly swirl around a central point. The stars form a shape that looks like water circling a drain. The pull of a black hole's gravity is one of the most powerful things in the universe. It sucks everything—even stars—down inside it. Scientists think that galaxies' shapes show that a black hole is at the center of each one, sucking the stars down inside. Hubble's images of galaxies have helped scientists find information for this idea.

Hubble has been in orbit for nearly 20 years. In 2018, the James Webb Space Telescope will be launched. It will be even more powerful than Hubble, and they will work together to solve the mysteries of our universe.

Circle the letter of the best answer to each question below.

1. The Hubble Space Telescope

   a. orbits Earth.

   b. orbits the sun.

   c. is on the moon's surface.

   d. is located at NASA headquarters.

2. The sun is part of

   a. Earth's orbit.

   b. the Milky Way galaxy.

   c. a black hole.

   d. the Eagle Nebula.

Write **true** or **false** next to each statement below.

3. _____ A nebula is a cloud of dust and gas.

4. _____ Comets usually orbit planets.

5. _____ Stars are made of galaxies.

6. _____ Black holes have very strong gravity.

Write your answers on the lines below.

7. Scientists think that black holes, which are invisible, are found at the centers of galaxies. Explain how scientists can tell that a black hole might be at a galaxy's center.

   _____

   _____

8. Explain why the Hubble Space Telescope can be more useful than a ground telescope.

   _____

   _____

What's Next?

Every 97 minutes, Hubble completes one orbit of Earth. Do some research to see many of the amazing images Hubble has made of galaxies, nebulae, and other space objects.

Review

Circle the letter of the best answer to each question below.

1. Stalagmites and stalactites found in caves are made of

   a. water.

   b. baking soda.

   c. minerals.

   d. soil.

2. Aluminum is

   a. human-made.

   b. the most common metal found in Earth's crust.

   c. also called *bauxite*.

   d. Both a and c

3. Air currents, or wind, are caused by

   a. differences in temperature.

   b. differences in pressure.

   c. Both a and b

   d. None of the above

4. What is a new moon?

   a. It's when the moon appears completely dark.

   b. It's another name for a full moon.

   c. It's when only a small amount of the moon can be seen.

   d. It's when the moon is nearly full.

5. Stars are formed inside

   a. black holes.

   b. planets.

   c. comets.

   d. nebulae.

Write your answers on the lines below.

6. Why is aluminum used on the outsides of many houses?

_____

7. Explain how clouds form.

_____

_____

8. Why are Uranus and Neptune known as the ice giants?

_____

9. Why don't icebergs sink?

_____

10. Name two lunar phases other than the full moon.

_____   _____

11. Why can life exist on Earth but not on the other planets in our solar system?

_____

12. Name one specific thing the Hubble Space Telescope has been used to study.

_____

Use the words in the box to complete the sentences below.

condenses	galaxies	evaporates	glacier	mined

13. When a chunk of ice breaks away from a _____ it's called *calving*.

14. Stalagmites and stalactites are formed when water _____ and leaves calcium behind.

15. The main reason bauxite is _____ is because it's a mineral that contains aluminum.

16. When the temperature drops, moisture in the air _____ around solid objects.

17. Most _____ contain millions of stars.

Lesson 5.1   Under Control

dams: barriers built across streams or rivers to keep water from flowing freely

reservoir: the pool of water that forms when water rises behind a dam

irrigate: to supply with water by artificial means

hydroelectric power: electricity made using the power of falling water

renewable: something in nature that continues to be produced; supplies are not limited

Other than the Great Wall of China, dams are the largest human-built structures in the world.

A temporary dam, called a *cofferdam*, is often built upstream from the construction of a dam. It blocks the flow of water long enough for the real dam to be built.

There are nearly 80,000 human-made dams in the United States.

The largest known beaver dams are more than 1,000 feet wide.

Why are dams built, and how do they work?

Many things in nature can't be controlled by human beings. For example, people don't have any way to control storms, wind, or the changing of the seasons. Water is a little different, though, because human beings do have some power over it.

Dams are built to control water flow in streams and rivers. The dammed-up water, called a **reservoir**, can be used for all sorts of things. It may be a source of drinking water, or it may be used to **irrigate**, or water, nearby farms. Some dams are used to control flooding. Dams are often great recreation areas. People use them for boating, swimming, and fishing.

Some dams are even used for **hydroelectric power**. That means that the energy from moving water is changed into electrical energy. Electrical energy is the energy used to power things in your home, like lights, the refrigerator, and the TV. Hydroelectric power is a **renewable** energy source. It's considered "clean," because it doesn't create air pollution or cause global warming.

A dam works by blocking or slowing the flow of water. The water pushes on the dam with a great deal of force. This water pressure means that dams must be very strong. Engineers decide what the best type of dam is for a particular place.

Embankment dams are the most common type in the United States. They are made of dirt and rock. They must be very thick so that water can't pass through them. Gravity dams are made of concrete. They are stronger, but they're also much more expensive to build. Both gravity and embankment dams use the force of their own weight to hold back the water.

Arch dams are usually built in narrow, rocky places, like canyons. The ends of the arch fit into notches in the canyon walls. Buttress dams are made of a slab of concrete that has supports, or buttresses, on one side. Because the wall has supports, it doesn't need to be as thick as the wall of a gravity dam. Less concrete can be used to build this type of dam.

Human beings aren't the only ones who build dams. Beavers are very talented dam builders in the natural world. Beaver dams are made of branches, logs, stones, and mud. Beavers build dams for protection from other animals, as well as to have a place to store their food for winter.

Circle the letter of the best answer to each question below.

1. Mr. Heigl and his team of engineers are going to build a dam in Pinevale Valley. There is not much space between the valley walls. Which type of dam is Mr. Heigl most likely to build?

   a. an embankment dam

   b. a gravity dam

   c. an arch dam

   d. a buttress dam

2. Gravity dams are

   a. less expensive to build than other types of dams.

   b. strong because they are built of concrete.

   c. no longer used because they burst too often.

   d. Both a and b

Write your answers on the lines below.

3. Name three purposes that dams serve.

   _____

   _____

4. What are two reasons why hydroelectric power is a good source of energy?

   _____

   _____

5. How are the dams of beavers different from the dams that human beings build?

   _____

   _____

6. How do dams create reservoirs?

   _____

   _____

exhale: to breathe out

regulate: to adjust the amount or rate of something at a certain level

micrometeoroids: tiny rocks that move at high speeds through space; also called *cosmic dust*

Early spacesuits were made especially for each astronaut. Today, the suits are made in pieces that fit together. Astronauts use the different parts to make suits that fit them.

On Earth, a modern spacesuit might weigh 280 pounds. How much do you think it weighs in space?

How do spacesuits keep astronauts safe in space?

If you live in a cold climate, you're probably used to bundling up in winter. Wearing many layers can make it hard to move around. This is similar to how it feels to wear a spacesuit. Most modern spacesuits have more than 10 layers of material. It sounds like a lot, but astronauts need to be protected from much more than just cold weather.

A spacesuit has a lot of jobs to do. Each must be done perfectly, or the astronaut wearing the suit could be in danger. There is little or no air pressure in space, so it's important that the spacesuit provides air pressure. Without it, the astronaut's body fluids would boil.

On Earth, the air is 78% nitrogen and 21% oxygen. In space, astronauts wear tanks in their backpacks that supply them with pure oxygen. They need to breathe pure oxygen for a couple of hours before they put on their suits to get all the nitrogen out of their systems. If they don't, they can get painful gas bubbles called the *bends*. They also need to have somewhere for the carbon dioxide to go when they **exhale**. Canisters in the suit take away the carbon dioxide before it reaches dangerous levels.

Temperatures in space can be extreme. Special fabrics and materials help keep astronauts at a comfortable temperature. Similar materials are often used in sports gear, such as running clothes or jackets for mountain climbers. Have you noticed that spacesuits are always white? The light color reflects sunlight, which also helps **regulate** the temperature inside the suit.

Small pieces of rock, called **micrometeoroids**, are always flying around in space. The materials used to create spacesuits must be tough enough to protect the wearer from these tiny rocks. It's also important that the material doesn't tear when the astronaut is exploring or working on a spacecraft.

The helmets of spacesuits are usually made of clear, heavy plastic. They may be tinted, like sunglasses, or have visors. They also have lights on them that the astronaut can direct into dark areas. Communication is important, so the astronauts wear radio headsets under their helmets. This allows them to talk with one another, as well as people on Earth.

They may be bulky and awkward to wear, but spacesuits are also an amazing piece of technology. With them, human beings have had the freedom to explore the universe.

Circle the letter of the best answer to each question below.

1. Why are spacesuits white, instead of a dark color, like black or navy blue?

   a. A dark suit would absorb light and make it warmer inside.

   b. White suits reflect sunlight, which makes it cooler inside.

   c. White suits are less expensive to make.

   d. Both a and b

2. The bends

   a. is an exercise that astronauts do.

   b. is a painful condition.

   c. are the places in a spacesuit that are most flexible.

   d. None of the above

Write your answers on the lines below.

3. How is the air that astronauts breathe in their spacesuits different from the air on Earth?

   _____

4. What are two ways in which a spacesuit protects an astronaut?

   _____

   _____

5. How has technology given astronauts more freedom in space?

   _____

6. How are spacesuits similar to some types of sports gear?

   _____

What's Next?

How have spacesuits changed over time? Technology has advanced, and so have spacesuits. Learn more about what the first spacesuits were like. What do scientists have planned for the future of space clothing?

You Won't Feel a Thing

general anesthesia: a drug that affects the whole body; it blocks pain and makes the patient unconscious

unconscious: a state of being asleep and unaware

anesthesiologist: a doctor who gives anesthesia and monitors the patient

monitor: to carefully watch over

local anesthesia: a drug that blocks pain in a certain area of the body

Acupuncture is an ancient Chinese medical practice. Thin, tiny needles are inserted into certain points on the body. Some people believe that this can block pain messages to the brain.

Dr. Crawford Long, a surgeon, first used ether in the early 1840s. He didn't share the results of his work, though, so others doctors didn't know about it. Dr. Morton was the first to publicly use ether and share his results. That's why he is often given credit as the first to use anesthesia.

What keeps people from feeling pain during surgery?

Before the mid-1800s, surgery wasn't very common. No one had yet discovered a way for patients to have surgery without pain. Lots of different methods had been tried. For example, painkillers made from plants were offered to the patient. Some healers tried to hypnotize patients. Other surgeons simply made the area numb with salt and ice. No matter what, surgery usually ended up being very painful. Some patients even died from the shock of the pain.

In October of 1846, medical history was made. The dentist William Morton gave a patient a chemical gas called *ether* before surgery. Doctors had experimented with gases before, but this was the first public demonstration. When the surgery was over and the patient woke up, he said he hadn't felt any pain. Anesthesia was born, and the world of medicine was changed forever.

Anesthesia affects the nervous system and keeps people from feeling pain. **General anesthesia** is used before major surgeries. It affects the brain cells, and the patient becomes **unconscious**. He or she isn't aware of what's happening, doesn't have any pain, and can't remember what happened afterward.

The drugs used in general anesthesia may be given in different ways—injected as a shot, inhaled as a gas, or pumped through a vein from an IV. Ether and chloroform were two of the earliest forms. There were risks to both, so people stopped using them when better choices were found.

During the surgery, the **anesthesiologist** uses machines to **monitor** a patient carefully. He or she makes sure that the patient's heart rate and breathing stay steady. The anesthesiologist must also make sure that the patient gets the right amount of anesthesia. It should last until the surgery is over, but not too much longer.

Local anesthesia affects only a certain area of the body. The drugs block the nerve cells in that part of the body from sending pain messages to the brain. If you've ever had a cavity filled, then you've probably had local anesthesia. The shot would have made your jaw and your cheek numb. You would not feel any pain while the dentist was drilling, but you'd be awake and you'd remember the experience.

Circle the letter of the best answer to each question below.

1. Mr. Cruz is going to have heart surgery on Thursday. He will probably have

   _____ before surgery.

   a. local anesthesia

   b. general anesthesia

   c. painkillers made from plants

   d. ether

2. A patient who has local anesthesia

   a. won't remember the procedure.

   b. will remember the procedure.

   c. will not experience the pain from the procedure.

   d. Both b and c

Write your answers on the lines below.

3. Anesthesia works by affecting the body's _____ system.

4. A person who has general anesthesia will be _____ during surgery.

5. Explain why local and not general anesthesia would be used when a patient is having a cavity filled.

   _____

   _____

6. Do you think the number of surgeries done today is greater or less than in the early 1800s? Why?

   _____

   _____

7. What does an anesthesiologist do?

   _____

   _____

A Moving Solution

carbon monoxide: poisonous gas produced by burning gasoline

limited resource: something that is useful but will not last forever

petroleum: also called *crude oil*; a natural resource used to make gasoline, plastics, and many other products

environment: Earth's entire ecosystem, including land, sea, and air

hybrid: containing the parts of more than one thing

Hybrid cars work best in the heavy traffic of a busy city. Cars in heavy traffic do a lot of accelerating and braking, so the hybrid will use and produce electricity. In places where cars travel long distances without stopping, like highways, hybrids use more gasoline.

Which is cleaner—electric power or gasoline power?

Every vehicle that uses gasoline leaves behind a trail of pollution. The white puffs of exhaust are easy to see when it's cold. In the summer, **carbon monoxide** is invisible. It's still there, though, as cars add poisonous chemicals to the air.

Soon after gasoline engines were invented, people could travel all over the planet. Products were quickly shipped from one place to another. The world you know today wouldn't exist without gasoline engines.

Today, we know that gasoline is a **limited resource**. Human beings use **petroleum** faster than it can be found. Its price keeps rising. The cost of gasoline comes in forms other than just money, though. Our **environment** also pays for some of our methods of travel. Oil spills, smog-covered cities, and global warming are just some of the ways our world has become less healthy. An important goal for the 21st century is finding cleaner ways to get around.

Electric cars are one possibility. They use electric motors instead of gas-burning engines. The motor gets its power from batteries. Electric cars are quiet. They don't produce exhaust. They also can't travel very far before running out of energy. Then, the cars need to be plugged into electrical outlets to recharge their batteries.

Hybrid cars are a more popular choice. They have two engines—a small gas engine and a larger electric motor. The clean, electric motor is used to get the car moving and during acceleration, which is when cars use the most energy. Once the car is rolling along, though, the gasoline engine takes over. A moving car needs only a small amount of power to keep moving, so the hybrid uses very little gas.

Hybrids can also make energy. When a hybrid slows down, the parts moving inside the engines have to slow down, too. This power, which was being used to move the car, can now be used to recharge the batteries. That's why hybrids don't need to be plugged in.

Hybrids still use gasoline, and someday we may need cars that don't use gasoline at all. Will these cars use solar energy? Nuclear energy? It could be an energy source we haven't even discovered yet. For now, though, walking and biking are the cleanest ways to travel.

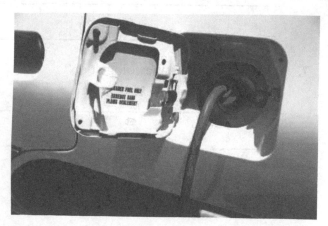

Circle the letter of the best answer to each question below.

1. Hybrid cars

   a. use electricity.

   b. burn gasoline.

   c. create energy.

   d. All of the above

2. A car uses the most energy when

   a. it's stopped.

   b. it's traveling at a steady speed.

   c. it's accelerating.

   d. it's braking.

Write **true** or **false** next to each statement below.

3. _____ Petroleum is a limited resource.

4. _____ Petroleum is made from gasoline.

5. _____ Hybrid cars do not produce any exhaust.

6. _____ Electric cars are quiet.

7. List two reasons someone might want to buy a hybrid car.

_____   _____

8. Why are hybrid cars more useful on city streets than on highways?

_____

_____

Unifying Concepts and Processes

Newton's first law of motion states that an object in motion tends to stay in motion. Explain how hybrid cars use this law.

_____

_____

Lighting the Future

filaments: thin wires inside incandescent light bulbs

efficient: able to do something with very little waste

Some people are hesitant to use CFLs because they cost much more to buy than regular light bulbs. However, it's estimated that each CFL will save you $30 by the time it burns out.

Try not to use CFLs in lights that are turned off and on many times a day because they won't last as long.

CFLs contain a tiny amount of mercury, which is a poison. You shouldn't throw CFLs in the trash. Instead, they should be recycled. Sometimes, you can recycle CFLs at the same store where you bought them.

How often do you need to change a light bulb?

For over a hundred years, most light bulbs have used **filaments** to create light. Filaments are short, thin wires inside light bulbs. When electricity passes through a filament, this wire gets very hot and begins glowing. The bulb fills with light and allows us to see in the dark. After a while, the filament breaks, and the bulb is burned out.

These kinds of light bulbs aren't very **efficient**. If you're lucky, they will burn for 1,000 hours before the filament breaks. That may seem like a long time, but it's actually only one and a half months. These bulbs have to be replaced quite often.

Today, a more efficient kind of light bulb is available. Compact fluorescent lights, or CFLs, don't use filaments. Fluorescent lights contain a gas that lights up when electricity is added to it. CFLs last more than ten times as long as regular light bulbs. However, CFLs also cost up to six times as much as a light bulb with a filament, making it much more expensive at first.

They also use a lot less electricity. Every time you turn on a light, you use electricity that was created at a power plant. Most power plants in the United States burn coal to produce electricity. All that burning coal creates pollution. The more electricity people use, the more pollution is created.

A CFL uses only one-quarter of the energy a regular light bulb uses, but it produces the same amount of light. In other words, a light bulb with a filament needs four times as much power as a CFL. That also means four times as much pollution, and four times as much money owed to the electric company. Switching to CFLs saves money and keeps the environment cleaner.

Many countries around the world are phasing out light bulbs with filaments. The United States completed its phaseout in 2014.

If everyone in the United States used just one CFL, it would mean 30 billion fewer tons of coal would be burned each year.

Circle the letter of the best answer to each question below.

1. Both CFLs and regular light bulbs use

   a. filaments.

   b. electricity.

   c. mercury.

   d. All of the above

2. CFL is short for

   a. cost-free light.

   b. coal-free lighting.

   c. compact fluorescent light.

   d. compact filament light.

Write **true** or **false** next to each statement below.

3. _____ CFLs cost more to buy than regular bulbs.

4. _____ The filament inside a CFL is made of gas.

5. _____ CFLs use a lot less energy than regular bulbs.

6. _____ Coal is burned to create electricity.

7. _____ CFLs last about twice as long as regular bulbs.

8. _____ CFLs are more efficient than regular bulbs.

Write your answer on the lines below.

9. Do you think it's a good idea to use CFLs instead of regular bulbs? Why or why not?

_____

_____

_____

_____

Farm-Fresh Milk

udders: the organs on a cow that produce and store milk

contaminates: makes impure or unusable

advances: progresses in development

Today, a very large dairy farm might have as many as 10,000 cows. It can take as little as an hour to milk 1,500 cows using high-tech modern machines. In that amount of time, they can produce 30,000 pounds of milk.

By 2005, more than 2,500 farms around the world used at least one AMS to milk their cows.

Cows have to be trained to use the AMS system. Often, rewards like fresh water or food are used to encourage them. Cows are also more comfortable after a milking, so they return to the milking shed more often.

How have milking machines changed dairy farms?

Most people have at least one dairy product—like milk, ice cream, cheese, butter, or yogurt—every day. Years ago, the milk would have come from a cow that was milked by hand. A dairy farmer could only have as many cows as he could milk twice in one day. A farmer couldn't skip a milking, so there wasn't much flexibility in his schedule.

Milk production has changed a lot over time. Most of the milk in grocery stores comes from large farms. These farms have too many cows to milk by hand. Instead, milking machines do almost all the work. Farm workers still need to clean the cows' **udders** first, so that no manure or dirt **contaminates** the milk. Then, workers connect cups to the udders. Once they've done this, the machine takes over. It uses a sort of vacuum to draw the milk out. The milk travels down a tube and into a collection bucket. Then, it is automatically pumped to a large vat.

Different systems are used to help the farm workers be efficient. For example, a rotary milking shed uses a huge turning platform. It has as many as 100 milking stalls on it. A motor rotates the platform, and after each cow is milked, it steps off the platform and another cow replaces it.

New **advances** in milking machines are being made all the time. Robotic milking is becoming common in many European countries. In this method, the cows decide when they are ready to be milked. They come to the milking shed, where they are recognized by a computer chip that has been placed under their skin. If it has been long enough since a cow was last milked, it is allowed to enter.

A robot arm does the job of a farm worker—it cleans the cow's udders and attaches the equipment. A computer records and stores information about each cow. When the udders are empty, a gate opens and the cow is sent back out to pasture. Cows can be milked at any time of day using the Automated Milking System (AMS), but only one cow can be milked at a time per machine. The farmer doesn't need to be there, though, since everything is run by a computer. This saves time and money.

Circle the letter of the best answer to each question below.

1. At the grocery store, it would be unusual to find

   a. milk from a cow that was milked by hand.

   b. milk from a cow that lives on a large dairy farm.

   c. milk from a cow that was milked by a machine.

   d. Both a and b

2. A cow's udders need to be washed before the cow is milked

   a. at least once a week.

   b. only when the cow is being milked by hand.

   c. or the cow will not produce any milk.

   d. to make sure that nothing gets into the milk.

Write **true** or **false** next to each statement below.

3. _____ A farm that uses an AMS does not need as many farm workers.

4. _____ Robots operate rotary milking sheds.

5. _____ Dairy farms today are very different than they were 100 years ago because of technology.

6. _____ Most cows do not need to be milked on a regular basis.

Write your answers on the lines below.

7. How do you think dairy farms would be different today if milking machines hadn't been invented?

   _____

8. What are two advantages of using an Automated Milking System?

   _____

   _____

9. When a farm uses an Automated Milking System, farm workers do not need to have contact with the cows on a daily basis. What would be a disadvantage of this? Explain.

   _____

   _____

Meals in Minutes

microwaves: short radio waves that are part of the electromagnetic spectrum

Metal should not be used in a microwave oven. It reflects microwaves, so they can't be absorbed by the food. It can also reflect the waves back into the magnetron and damage it.

The ability of microwaves to cook food was discovered by accident. In 1945, Percy Spencer was experimenting with using microwaves in radar. He noticed that a candy bar in his pocket melted when he was near the magnetron. Then, he experimented with unpopped corn. You can guess the results! His discovery led to the creation of the first microwave oven. It was 6 feet tall and weighed 750 pounds!

How do microwave ovens do their job so quickly?

You come home from a softball game on Saturday afternoon. You're starving, so you pop a frozen pizza in the microwave. A few minutes later, you're biting into a steamy hot meal. How did the microwave cook a piece of frozen food so quickly? It would have taken much longer in a conventional, or regular, oven.

Microwave ovens heat food differently than conventional ovens. They use **microwaves**, which are very short radio waves. They are absorbed by water, fats, and sugars. These waves are not absorbed by most other materials, like plastic, ceramic, or glass. When you heat food in a microwave, only the food is heated—the container, the air inside the oven, and the oven itself are not heated. A dish might be warm when you take it out of the microwave, but the oven didn't heat it. The microwaves heated the food. Then, the heat traveled from the food into the dish.

When you close the door to a microwave oven and turn it on, a device called a *magnetron* produces microwaves. Spinning metal blades scatter the microwaves through the oven. The food absorbs these waves. They cause the molecules in the food, especially water molecules, to start moving around very quickly. The faster a substance's molecules are moving, the hotter it is. These quickly moving molecules cook the food.

Microwaves would be dangerous if they escaped the oven. This is why microwave ovens don't work unless the door is tightly sealed. The glass in the door lets the user keep an eye on the food as it cooks. A fine layer of mesh in the glass stops most of the microwaves from passing through it.

Have you ever noticed that foods cook differently in a microwave than they do in a regular oven? Breads and pastries, especially, become soft and never get a crispy outer layer. In a conventional oven, the air becomes very hot and dry. This causes moisture on the outside of food to evaporate. It makes the crust crunchy on a loaf of bread, while the inside stays soft. In a microwave oven, the air isn't heated. The outside of a microwaved bagel or roll isn't any different than the inside.

About 95% of American homes have microwave ovens. Microwave ovens cook food quickly and efficiently, and they save people time.

Circle the letter of the best answer to each question below.

1. Which of the following would absorb microwaves?

    a. a ceramic mug

    b. a blueberry muffin

    c. a plastic plate

    d. Both a and c

2. Using metal in a microwave can

    a. cause foods to cook more quickly.

    b. help food brown better.

    c. keep breads from forming a crusty layer outside.

    d. damage the magnetron.

Write your answers on the lines below.

3. What effect do microwaves have on molecules? How does this cause food to cook?

    _____

    _____

4. Luis decided to heat up some leftovers for lunch. When he took the ceramic plate out of the microwave, he burned his hand on it. Ceramic doesn't absorb microwaves, so how did this happen?

    _____

    _____

5. Jessy wants to bake a loaf of bread. Should she use a microwave or a regular oven? Why?

    _____

    _____

Unifying Concepts and Processes

Do you think Percy Spencer was a good scientist? Explain your answer.

_____

_____

Review

Circle the letter of the best answer to each question below.

1. General anesthesia

   a. blocks pain from one specific part of the body.

   b. blocks pain in the entire body.

   c. allows a patient to remember the procedure.

   d. Both b and c

2. Using CFLs can

   a. reduce the amount of coal that is burned.

   b. help people save money.

   c. reduce the amount of electricity people use.

   d. All of the above

3. Which of the following is not a fossil fuel?

   a. petroleum

   b. coal

   c. electricity

   d. natural gas

4. Food cooked in a microwave oven _____ microwaves.

   a. absorbs

   b. reflects

   c. produces

   d. damages

Write your answers on the lines below.

5. What are two uses for dams?

   _____

   _____

6. Why is hydroelectric power considered a clean source of energy?

   _____

7. Spacesuits provide astronauts with oxygen. They also need to remove the air the astronaut exhales. Explain why.

_____

_____

_____

8. Explain why surgery became more common once anesthesia started being used.

_____

_____

9. Why is burning fossil fuels bad for the environment?

_____

_____

10. Why do hybrid cars use less gasoline than regular cars?

_____

11. Explain why CFLs should not be thrown into the trash.

_____

12. How do you think milking machines have changed the lives of farmers?

_____

13. How do microwave ovens cook food?

_____

Write **true** or **false** next to each statement below.

14. _____ Some types of dams use the force of their own weight to hold back water.

15. _____ Spacesuits need to provide air pressure because the air pressure in space is much higher than it is on Earth.

16. _____ Hybrid cars get their power only from electricity.

17. _____ CFLs cost more to buy than regular light bulbs.

18. _____ You should never place anything made of metal in a microwave.

Lesson 6.1 — A Body of Water

dehydrated: low on water or body fluids

photosynthesis: the chemical process that allows plants to make food

digest: to break food down into simple forms that the body can use

Water doesn't just help with digestion. It's in your blood, helping to move oxygen around your body. Water also plays a big role in the lymphatic system, which helps your body fight disease.

Drinks like soda and sweet juices aren't good sources of the liquids your body needs. Many sodas contain caffeine, and caffeine causes your body to lose water. Some juices have a lot of extra sugar. These sugars have to be digested, and your body uses up water to break them down. The best way to get hydrated is to drink water.

Why is water so important for life?

When you're hot and sweaty, nothing tastes better than a cold glass of water. Part of the reason it tastes so good is that your body is glad to have it. Exercise and hot weather can make you **dehydrated**. It's important to drink plenty of water every day, but you should drink even more when it's hot out.

The human body needs a lot of water—almost two-thirds of your body's mass is made up of water. This water doesn't just sit there, though. Your body uses it to keep you alive. In fact, all life on Earth depends on liquid water.

Water is a powerful chemical. It can break apart the molecules of many other chemicals. Water is used in many of the chemical reactions that keep organisms alive. For example, plants need water for **photosynthesis**. Water mixes with carbon dioxide and sunlight to cause a chemical reaction. This process is how plants make their food.

Animals don't use water to make their food, but they use water to help **digest** the food inside their bodies. Food contains sugars and fats that are made of big, complicated molecules. The chemicals your body needs are hidden inside those sugar and fat molecules. Water breaks down the big molecules into simpler ones that your body can use.

Water also removes waste products from your body. When you go to the bathroom, water gets rid of the chemicals that your body doesn't need. If you don't have enough water, these waste chemicals can build up inside your body and make you sick.

Sweating and going to the bathroom cause you to lose water. You even lose water just by breathing. Exhale onto a mirror, and you can see the water in your breath condense on the glass. You must replace the water your body loses as it works through the day.

The amount of water you need changes from day to day. If it's hot outside and you're playing really hard, you should drink a lot of water. On a lazy Saturday in the middle of winter, however, you might not need as much. On average, you should have about six cups of liquid each day. Some of this liquid can come from food, milk, and juices, too.

Circle the letter of the best answer to the question below.

1. What happens if you don't drink enough water?

   a. You can gain weight.

   b. You can become dehydrated.

   c. You can suffer from photosynthesis.

   d. All of the above

2. Water is a type of

   a. chemical.

   b. sugar.

   c. fat.

   d. Both a and b

3. Water is important for all organisms because

   a. it helps produce chemical reactions that keep organisms live.

   b. it helps living things make or digest food.

   c. it carries chemicals out of organisms' bodies.

   d. All of the above

Write your answers on the lines below.

4. List three ways that water leaves your body.

   _____

5. How does your body let you know you need water?

   _____

6. Explain why soda and sugary juices aren't the best drink choices when you are dehydrated.

   _____

   _____

7. Why should you drink more water when you exercise?

   _____

   _____

recommendations: guidelines

calcium: a chemical element found in milk, bone, and shells; necessary for bone health

protein: foods like meat, beans, and fish that your body uses as building blocks for muscle, skin, and bones

lean: having little or no fat

The wedges of the pyramid are different sizes. That's because you should eat more of some foods in each group than others. For example, a little juice is okay, as long as it doesn't contain sugar, but whole fruits are better for you.

A figure climbing stairs is pictured on one side of the pyramid. The USDA added this symbol of exercise because no matter how well you eat, your body still needs exercise to stay healthy. Kids should try to get about 60 minutes of exercise on most days.

What should you eat every day to feel healthy and stay fit?

Everyone knows that you need to eat well to have a healthy body and feel good. Your parents probably remind you to eat your veggies and not fill up on junk food. But do you know what the best foods are for you to eat every day? And how do you know how much of each type of food to eat?

In 2005, the United States Department of Agriculture (USDA) released a new food pyramid called MyPyramid. It divides food into categories and gives people **recommendations** for how to eat well. People are different, which means that their nutritional needs are different (depending on age, activity level, weight, etc.)

A wide orange wedge on the pyramid symbolizes grains. They can be found in breads, pasta, and cereals. Generally, however, at least half the grains you eat each day should be whole grains. On a list of ingredients, the first word should be *whole*. Your diet should also include $2\frac{1}{2}$ cups of vegetables and $1\frac{1}{2}$ cups of fruit a day. Try to choose foods that have a variety of colors, like dark green spinach, bright red strawberries, and deep orange sweet potatoes. Fruits and veggies that have dark, rich colors contain the most vitamins and minerals.

Milk is so important that it has a category all to itself—the blue wedge on the pyramid. You need three cups of milk a day. It contains **calcium**, which helps you grow and builds strong bones. Cheese and yogurt are included in the milk group—just make sure they are low-fat or fat-free.

Meat, beans, and oils take up less space on the pyramid because you don't need as much of them as you do of other foods. You should eat about five ounces of **protein**—like fish, chicken, peanut butter, and peas—a day. Choose **lean** proteins when you can. Your body needs some fat to work properly, but you should limit the amount of oils you eat. Remember that the fats from fish and nuts are more healthful. Liquid oils, like canola or olive oil, are better for you than solid fats, like butter.

At the tip of MyPyramid, there is a small white spot. It's the symbol for foods that you eat that don't fit into the other categories. Sugary snacks and pop fit into this area. It's a pretty small spot, though, which means you better make sure this type of food is only an occasional treat.

MyPyramid.gov
STEPS TO A HEALTHIER YOU

Look at each pair of foods listed below. Make a check mark next to the food that is the more healthful, better choice in each pair.

1. _____ light-green iceberg lettuce _____ dark green spinach

2. _____ low-fat strawberry yogurt _____ a strawberry milkshake

3. _____ an orange _____ a glass of grape juice

4. _____ white toast with butter _____ whole-wheat toast with peanut butter

5. _____ a piece of lean chicken _____ a piece of fried chicken

Write your answers on the lines below.

6. What is the purpose of MyPyramid?

_____

7. What does the white spot at the top of the pyramid stand for, and why is it so small?

_____

_____

8. If you eat six ounces of grains a day, how much should be whole grains?

_____

9. Why are dairy products an important part of a healthy diet?

_____

10. MyPyramid is a food guide, so why are there stairs along one side of it?

_____

What's Next?

MyPyramid is different for people of different ages. An active child will have different recommendations than a college student or a grandparent. Visit www.mypyramid.gov to get a plan that is right for your age, height, weight, gender, and level of activity.

viruses: tiny particles that cause disease and illness

reproducing: making more of the same kind

immune system: the body's system for fighting illness and disease

infect: make sick or pass along an illness

symptoms: signs or evidence of an illness

evolve: to change from one form into another stronger or more advanced form

Scientists aren't sure whether to call viruses "living organisms" or not. Viruses don't have cells, which are the building blocks of living things. They also don't reproduce on their own. A virus needs to use the body of a living organism to make copies of itself. Viruses do evolve, though, which is a characteristic of living things.

If you have a fever along with cold symptoms, you might have the flu. The flu is a more serious infection, so you should see a doctor.

Why is there no cure for the common cold?

Your head hurts. You can't stop coughing. Your nose runs, but you can't breathe through it either. Every time you swallow, it hurts your throat. You keep sneezing. No doubt about it, having a cold isn't fun. Unfortunately, we all get sick once in a while.

Most people catch colds a couple of times each year. Children can get sick many more times than that, though. Hundreds of kids spending the day together at school helps colds spread quickly from child to child.

Colds are caused by **viruses**. A virus is a tiny particle that causes infection. When a virus enters your body, it begins **reproducing** quickly. Soon, your body's **immune system** is hard at work fighting the tiny invaders.

Cold viruses **infect** the area between your nose and throat. Sneezing, coughing, and a running nose are just your body trying to get rid of the virus. The virus also uses these **symptoms** to move from one body into another.

When people sneeze or rub their noses, viruses get onto their hands. If they don't wash their hands, then the virus will end up on whatever they touch. A cold virus can live for five hours or more on smooth things like door handles and counters. When another person comes along and touches the same spot, the virus will end up on his or her hand. Cold viruses usually get into a body through the eyes or nose. If you have a virus on your hand, then touching your face can end up making you sick.

Luckily, the human body does a pretty good job of fighting cold viruses. Your immune system usually kills off the viruses in just a few days. Your body remembers each virus, too. The same virus will never infect you more than once. Viruses can survive only by finding new people to infect.

Unfortunately, you'll never become immune to every cold virus. There are hundreds of different kinds. Cold viruses **evolve** quickly, too. New ones are always showing up.

You can prevent colds by keeping the viruses from spreading. Washing your hands is the best way to do this. Use soap, and rub your hands together under warm, running water. The viruses won't be killed, but the rubbing gets them off your hands.

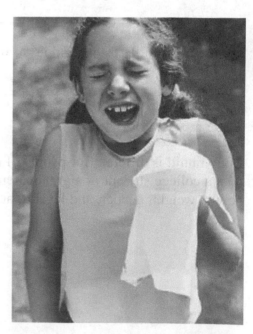

Circle the letter of the best answer to each question below.

1. The best way to prevent colds from spreading is to

    a. take medicine.

    b. wash your hands.

    c. cough and sneeze.

    d. Both a and b

2. Your immune system

    a. keeps viruses from getting into your body.

    b. is located in between your nose and throat.

    c. fights viruses that have entered your body.

    d. All of the above

Write your answers on the lines below.

3. In your own words, explain how viruses travel from one person to another.

    _____

    _____

    _____

4. Why do you think there is no cure for the common cold?

    _____

    _____

5. Bacteria are tiny, living organisms. They can cause illness. Why don't antibacterial soaps help prevent the spread of colds?

    _____

    _____

What's Next?

Rhinoviruses—*rhino* is Greek for "nose"—are the most common viruses that infect human beings. They cause most of the colds we get. Viruses are responsible for many other illnesses, too. Some of these viruses have caused epidemics. What is an epidemic, and what viruses have caused them?

The Problem with Plastic

prehistoric: long before human beings began recording history

extract: to pull out or remove

durable: long-lasting; hard to break

degrade: break down complicated chemicals into simpler ones

recycled: used again

Plastics are made from petroleum. Just like other petroleum products, like gasoline, plastics contain usable energy. In some places, plastic waste isn't recycled into more plastic. Instead, it's burned to produce power for the local community.

Scientists have tried creating plastics that will break down more quickly. One of the most successful ideas has been plastic that breaks down in a few days when left in the sun.

Why is it wasteful to throw away plastic?

Fossil fuels, like coal and petroleum, took millions of years to form. They're made from **prehistoric** plants and animals that died and were slowly covered by rocks and mud. Deep underground, the extreme heat and pressure cooked the remains for millions of years. Today, human beings **extract** these fossil fuels from the ground and burn them for energy.

Petroleum, which is used to make gasoline, is also used to make plastic. Every time you drink from a plastic bottle, you're holding something that took millions of years to be made.

Plastic is a very **durable** material. Your plastic bottle—and millions like it—will take at least a hundred years to **degrade** so that Earth can use its chemicals again. Plastics might even sit in landfills for a thousand years. No one knows for sure because plastic was invented only about a hundred years ago.

Today, many kinds of plastics can be **recycled**. Plastic bottles, bags, and other containers are taken to recycling plants, where they are shredded into small pieces. These pieces are melted down and used to make new plastic products. Picnic tables, trashcans, garbage bags, and carpeting are just some of the items that can be made from recycled plastic.

One problem with recycling plastics is that you can't mix different kinds together. To help with this problem, a code was invented. On almost every plastic container—usually on the bottom—you will find a small triangle with a number inside. This number tells you what kind of plastic it is. If you see the numbers 1 or 2 in the triangle, don't throw the container in the trash. These are the two kinds of plastic that are easiest to recycle. Look for a recycling bin to throw the container into. You can also collect a bunch of number 1 and 2 plastics and take them to a nearby recycling center.

Americans recycle about 80 percent of their newspapers and about 70 percent of their cardboard. Only about five percent of plastics are recycled, though. For a long time, plastic was very cheap to produce. As the price of petroleum keeps going up, plastic is becoming more expensive. Someday, recycled plastic could be the main source of the plastics we use.

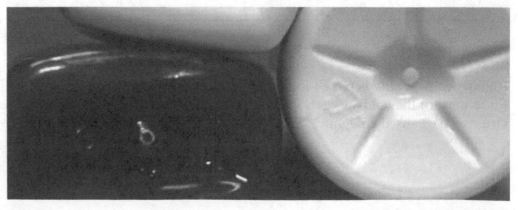

Circle the letter of the best answer to each question below.

1. Plastic is made from

    a. petroleum.

    b. fossil fuel.

    c. gasoline.

    d. Both a and b

2. It takes _____ for a piece of plastic to degrade.

    a. about one year

    b. about ten years

    c. hundreds of years

    d. No one knows for sure

Write your answer on the lines below.

3. Why are so many products made from plastic?

    _____

4. Besides recycling, what is another way old plastic can be made useful?

    _____

5. Why does the author think that throwing plastic into the garbage is wasteful?

    _____

6. Paper or plastic? It takes a lot less energy to make a plastic bag than it does to make a paper bag. Plastic bags are made of petroleum, which is a nonrenewable resource. Paper comes from trees, which are renewable resources. Both paper and plastic can be recycled, although people are much better about recycling paper. Which kind of bag would you choose and why?

    _____

    _____

breeding: reproducing; having young

trawlers: large fishing boats that drag nets along the ocean floor

moratorium: a temporary stop to something

overfished: fished too heavily in one area, so that populations of fish are changed

Most of the cod caught by foreign boats was salted and dried, which made it last a long time. When people were ready to eat it, they could soak it in water before cooking it so that it would plump up again.

Cod is a popular fish because of its mild flavor and lean, flaky white meat. If you've ever ordered fish and chips at a restaurant, you've probably eaten cod.

Almost all of a cod's fat is stored in its liver. It's used to make cod liver oil— a supplement that some people take for its vitamins and healthy fats.

Why have the numbers of cod in Canadian waters dropped so sharply?

Newfoundland is an island off the east coast of Canada. When European explorers first discovered it in the 15th century, they were amazed by the amount of cod in its waters. People said they could simply dip baskets into the ocean and bring them up full of fish. For centuries, large European boats traveled to Newfoundland to fish.

For hundreds of years, the eastern Canadian waters were fished heavily. Still, there seemed to be plenty of cod. A large female cod can lay as many as five million eggs over the course of a lifetime. There were always enough **breeding** fish left to keep the cod population healthy.

All that changed in the 1950s and 1960s. Huge fishing **trawlers** came from foreign countries. The fisherman worked in shifts so that they could fish 24 hours a day. In an hour, they could catch 200 tons of cod. That's more than the early ships might catch in a whole season. The fish were frozen right away, so they would stay fresh for the trip home.

Over the next few decades, the number of cod dropped steadily. Canada put a limit on how close to its shores foreign boats could fish. Still, the large Canadian trawlers continued to damage the ocean floor by dragging their weighted nets. Even though there were fewer cod left, the fisherman were better at finding them. Technology, like sonar and satellite images, helped them track the remaining fish. The number of cod kept dropping.

By 1992, levels of cod were lower than they had ever been. If something didn't change, the fish would completely disappear. The Canadian government called a **moratorium**, or a temporary stop, to cod fishing in the waters off Newfoundland. Between 30,000 and 40,000 people lost jobs. Scientists don't know yet whether the number of cod will ever rise to the levels they once were.

When an area is **overfished**, it causes changes to the ecosystem. For example, if a top predator fish, like cod, is removed, other fish will take its place. Even if young cod are allowed to breed again, they may never get their place back at the top of the food chain. Each level of the food chain is affected. The balance is very fragile. Once it gets thrown off, it's hard to know if it will ever be able to right itself.

Circle the letter of the best answer to each question below.

1. Why did Europeans come to Newfoundland to fish?

   a. There was a shortage of fish in Europe.

   b. There was a huge supply of cod in Newfoundland.

   c. Fishing wasn't allowed in European waters.

   d. Both a and b

2. Why didn't the supply of cod drop too low before fishing trawlers were used?

   a. Because older fishing methods damaged the ocean floor

   b. Because the fishermen were careful not to remove too many fish from the sea

   c. Because the fishermen didn't catch as many fish

   d. Both a and c

3. Which of the following statements is not true?

   a. Many people lost their jobs when a stop was put to cod fishing in Canada.

   b. The meat of a cod is lean because most of the fish's fat is stored in its liver.

   c. Overfishing does not have any effect on marine ecosystems.

   d. Female cod lay millions of eggs.

Write your answers on the lines below.

4. Why did the Canadian government call a moratorium on cod fishing?

   _____

5. Will there ever be large numbers of cod again in Canada's eastern waters?

   _____

6. What effect did huge fishing trawlers have on Canada's cod?

   _____

   _____

7. How was cod preserved for the journey home by early fishermen?

   _____

The Nuclear Option

atomic: having to do with atoms

reactors: devices that control nuclear energy

radioactive: giving off rays or waves of energy that comes from atoms

alternative: choice, option, or selection

Accidents at nuclear power plants can be very destructive and deadly. In 1986, the Chernobyl Nuclear Power Plant, located in the Ukraine, exploded when steam caused too much pressure. Large amounts of radiation escaped from the plant. Hundreds of thousands of people were removed from the area. Today, the city of Chernobyl is still mostly abandoned.
In 2001, the Fukushima 1 Nuclear Power Plant in Japan had a catastrophic failure after the plant was hit by a tsunami. The resulting meltdown was the second worst nuclear incident after Chernobyl. Cleanup is expected to take decades.

There are more than one hundred nuclear power plants in the United States. They provide Americans with about 20 percent of their electricity.

How safe are nuclear power plants?

In the 1940s, a new source of energy was discovered—**atomic** power. There is a huge amount of energy stored inside every atom. Scientists found a way to break atoms apart and release this energy. During the 1950s, nuclear **reactors** were designed that took the energy and made it useful to human beings. Nuclear power plants were built around the world. People saw them as a clean solution to the world's energy needs, mostly because nuclear reactors don't create smoke.

Unfortunately, atomic energy has other dangers. The fuel used in nuclear reactors is **radioactive**. Like ultraviolet light from the sun, radiation is invisible and odorless, but it can burn you and give you cancer. Nuclear fuels are very dangerous.

Nuclear waste—made when the fuel is no longer useful—is even deadlier. It has to be buried deep underground so human beings never come in contact with it. Nuclear waste remains dangerous for thousands of years.

People have argued for a long time about whether nuclear power is a good or bad **alternative** to other energy sources. Most of the energy human beings use comes from burning fossil fuels. Coal is burned to create electricity. Petroleum is burned to get us from place to place. Natural gas is burned to keep us warm. Fossil fuels are useful, but they aren't very good for the environment. For a long time, people have known that burning fossil fuels pollutes the air. Today, most scientists think that pollution is causing Earth's oceans and atmosphere to warm up.

Nuclear power doesn't pollute the air or change Earth's temperature. Nuclear fuels are also much cheaper than fossil fuels. Uranium—the metal that's used as nuclear fuel—doesn't cost very much. Nuclear reactors are expensive to build, though. They have to have very thick walls to keep heat and radiation from escaping. After the reactor is built, it produces a lot of energy from only a small amount of material.

Even some people who used to think nuclear power was too dangerous are changing their minds today. Which is more dangerous to life on Earth, they wonder—global warming caused by fossil fuels or nuclear waste? Others think that's the wrong question. They believe the answer lies in alternative energy sources like solar and wind power. These are both clean and renewable ways of getting power.

Circle the letter of the best answer to each question below.

1. Nuclear power is created by

   a. burning atoms.

   b. breaking atoms apart.

   c. melting uranium.

   d. burning radiation.

2. Radiation

   a. looks like fog or steam.

   b. is invisible.

   c. smells like gas.

   d. Both b and c

3. What happens when nuclear waste is buried in the ground?

   a. It becomes safe.

   b. There's no light, so the radiation isn't very strong.

   c. It remains dangerous and radioactive for thousands of years.

   d. Both a and b

Write your answers on the lines below.

4. After reading this selection, do you think nuclear energy is a good or bad idea? Explain your answer.

   _____

   _____

   _____

   _____

What's Next?

Where does the power you use come from? Visit the Web site for the electric company that serves your area. It will list their power plants and show you where they are located. Are any of them near your home? Some of your electricity may even come from an alternative source, like wind power.

The Great Stink

sanitary: free from dirt, infection, or anything that might cause illness

cholera: disease that causes vomiting and diarrhea

sewage: waste that is carried away by sewers

engineer: a person who designs and builds things

Cholera is caused by bacteria that live in unclean water.

Although the ocean is huge, dumping sewage into it can still cause problems. Like human beings, fish and other marine animals can get sick from the bacteria that live in waste. Ocean tides and currents can bring the waste right back to shore. Swimming in unclean water can make people sick.

Today, we treat sewage at treatment plants before water is sent back into Earth's waterways. Filters, chemicals, and even bacteria are used to break down sewage and create clean water.

What happens when a million people need to use the bathroom?

In the early 1800s, a new invention started to enter the homes of London, England. It was the toilet. Until then, people used outhouses or chamber pots.

An outhouse was a small shed built over a deep hole. Waste dropped into the hole, but sooner or later, the hole filled up. Someone had to clean it out. Chamber pots were used indoors. These small containers had to be emptied after every use. The contents were often dumped into the streets. Whether waste came from under an outhouse or it drained off the streets, it all ended up in London's streams and rivers.

Toilets made London's homes more **sanitary**. Waste no longer sat around in pots or holes in the ground. It was flushed away as soon as it appeared. Of course, the waste didn't just disappear. It still ended up in London's waterways.

The River Thames flows through the middle of London. More than a million people lived in London during the mid-1800s. All their waste drained into the Thames. A million people need a lot of drinking water, too, which also came from the Thames.

In 1849 and 1854, **cholera** epidemics spread through London. Thousands of people died. A report showed that dirty water in the Thames was causing this disease. Still, nothing was done to solve the problem. Waste continued filling the Thames. It was a poisonous river.

The summer of 1858 was very warm. The river already smelled bad, but with the hot weather, London filled with an awful odor. England's leaders hung curtains soaked in chemicals over the windows of the House of Commons. People could hardly step outside. That summer became known as "The Great Stink." Finally, everyone knew something had to be done.

More than a decade earlier, the artist John Martin had designed a sewer system for London. Instead of dumping **sewage** straight into the river, it would be held in giant reservoirs. From there, the waste could be drained into the ocean—not dumped back into London's drinking water. Martin's idea was used to solve the pollution problem.

Engineer Joseph Bazalgette led the effort to complete this huge project. Thousands of miles of sewers below London's streets were designed to flow to the reservoirs. It took several years and a lot of money, but people stopped getting sick. And London never smelled so bad again.

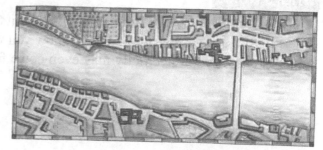

Circle the letter of the best answer to each question below.

1. The River Thames became polluted because

    a. a million people lived in London.

    b. toilets had just been invented.

    c. there wasn't a good system for getting rid of waste.

    d. it didn't flow quickly enough.

2. Why were people getting sick with cholera?

    a. They were using unclean toilets.

    b. Their drinking water was polluted.

    c. They used outhouses and chamber pots.

    d. The sewers were clogged.

3. Waste from outhouses and chamber pots was

    a. flushed down the toilet.

    b. collected by people who took it to the ocean.

    c. buried underground.

    d. dumped into London's waterways.

Write your answers on the lines below.

4. What two things caused "The Great Stink" of 1858?

    _____   _____

5. How did dumping sewage into the ocean solve London's problem? Why wasn't it the best solution?

    _____

    _____

Unifying Concepts and Processes

Treatment plants are usually built where a river flows away from a city. Why does the dirty water still need to be treated, even though it will be flowing away from the city?

    _____

    _____

NAME _____

Review

Circle the letter of the best answer to each question below.

1. If you are exercising, what's your best drink option?

   a. sweetened juice

   b. water

   c. soda

   d. iced tea

2. Colds are caused by

   a. bacteria.

   b. viruses.

   c. vaccines.

   d. All of the above

3. Look for a number in a _____ to see what kind of plastic something is made of.

   a. circle

   b. square

   c. triangle

   d. green box

4. The "Great Stink" was caused by

   a. pollution in the River Thames.

   b. hot weather.

   c. acid rain.

   d. Both a and b

Write your answers on the lines below.

5. The plastics that are easiest to recycle are symbolized by the numbers _____ and _____ .

6. What's the best way to avoid catching a cold?

   _____

7. Why do the recommendations of MyPyramid change from one person to another?

   _____

8. Why are the wedges for proteins and oils smaller than the other wedges on MyPyramid?

_____

9. List two ways your body uses water.

_____   _____

10. List two ways your body loses water.

_____   _____

11. Name one similarity and one difference between bacteria and viruses.

_____

_____

12. Cod aren't fished as heavily as they once were. Why is there still a chance that their populations won't recover?

_____

13. What is one danger of using atomic energy?

_____

14. What is one advantage to using atomic energy?

_____

15. Why is it important to clean waste water before sending it back into Earth's waterways?

_____

Read each sentence below. Underline the correct answer from the two choices.

16. The most nutritious fruits and vegetables are the ones that are the (most, least) colorful.

17. Cold viruses (evolve, infect) the area between the nose and throat.

18. Plastic is made from (gasoline, petroleum).

19. (Technology, Trawlers) damaged the marine ecosystems where cod lived.

20. Atomic energy is (an alternative, a solution) to fossil fuels.

21. The (bacteria, cholera) epidemics in London were caused by dirty drinking water.

| Lesson 7.1 | The Roots of Science |

contributions: things that a person or group has to offer others

anatomy: the structure of living things

dissecting: cutting open for scientific observation

Archimedes came up with a theory of buoyancy, or why things float. A story often told is that he came up with this theory in the bathtub! The king was worried that his new crown was not solid gold and asked for Archimedes' help. One day, when Archimedes got into a bath, the water overflowed. He figured out that the amount of what that overflowed was equal to his weight in water. He knew that he could place the crown in some water and see how much overflowed. If it equaled the amount of water that overflowed when a chunk of pure gold of the same weight was placed in the water, then the crown was truly all gold.

What kind of understanding did the early Greeks have of science?

Scientific knowledge and understanding don't happen all at once. Scientists build on each other's ideas. Even ideas that don't turn out to be correct are important. They are part of the process that leads scientists to a better understanding of our world and the universe. Think of each idea, theory, or experiment as a building block. Each new layer of blocks builds upon the last.

The ancient Greeks made many **contributions** to the world of science. They observed the world around them and carefully recorded their observations and their ideas. The scientist Democritus was an advanced thinker for his time. He believed that everything is made of tiny particles, or atoms. He said that the atoms could combine to form new substances. Even though Democritus lived more than 2,000 years ago, his ideas about atoms weren't very different from what we know to be true today.

Early Greek astronomers thought that Earth was at the center of the universe. They believed that the sun and planets moved around Earth. Aristarchus, a Greek astronomer, felt sure that this was wrong. He believed that Earth and the planets revolved around the sun. Few people agreed with Aristarchus or Democritus at the time. Even so, later scientists found these early Greeks to be correct in their beliefs.

Hipparchus was another important Greek astronomer. He named more than 800 stars during his lifetime. Ptolemy built upon many of Hipparchus's ideas. He wrote a 13-volume book called the *Almagest*. It included everything the Greeks knew about astronomy at the time.

Medical science of the early Greeks wasn't very advanced. People thought illness was a punishment from the Greek gods. Hippocrates, a doctor, didn't believe this. He knew that there were scientific reasons why people became sick. He opened the door for others to begin looking for the causes of diseases. Years later, doctors like Herophilus and Erasistratus learned much more about human **anatomy** and disease by **dissecting**, or cutting open, the bodies of people who had died. This helped them see how the body works and how disease affected it.

The Greeks were curious, critical thinkers. The knowledge they passed on helped build the foundation of modern science. How different would the world of science be today without the ancient Greeks?

Circle the letter of the best answer to each question below.

1. Democritus's ideas about atoms were

    a. similar to modern ideas about atoms.

    b. completely incorrect.

    c. accepted by most other Greeks.

    d. not new or original.

2. The early Greeks believed that _____ caused illness.

    a. bacteria

    b. atoms

    c. the stars

    d. the Greek gods

Write **true** or **false** next to each statement below.

3. _____ Seeing inside the human body helped the ancient Greeks learn about disease.

4. _____ Hippocrates believed it was necessary to look for the causes of illness.

Write your answers on the lines below.

5. How were Aristarchus's ideas about the universe different from what most Greeks thought at the time?

    _____

    _____

6. In the story of Archimedes, how could he tell whether the king's crown was really solid gold?

    _____

    _____

Unifying Concepts and Processes

Using the ancient Greeks as an example, explain why it is important for scientists to share the results of their work.

_____

_____

The Parents of Chemistry

colleague: a partner or associate in a profession

respiration: the process that organisms use to bring oxygen into their bodies

complex: having many detailed or complicated parts

elements: substances that contain only one kind of atom

Many historians believe that Marie Lavoisier was an essential partner in her husband's scientific work. Antoine got all the credit for their discoveries, though, because it wasn't proper in those days for women to work in science. It would be another hundred years before women became common members of the scientific community. Florence Nightingale, Elizabeth Blackwell, Marie Curie, and Beatrix Potter were just some of the female scientists working in the late 1800s.

Beatrix Potter was best known for her books about Peter Rabbit, but she was also a mycologist— a scientist who studies mushrooms and other fungi.

Who discovered the elements?

Chemistry is the science of chemical reactions. It looks at how molecules change or stay the same when they are mixed with other molecules. A Frenchman named Antoine Lavoisier is often called the "father of modern chemistry."

Lavoisier lived in France during the 1700s. His contributions to science are some of the greatest ever made. Lavoisier also showed the world how a carefully controlled experiment could answer a scientific question.

During his short life, Lavoisier always worked with his **colleague** and wife, Marie Lavoisier. She helped Antoine plan the experiments and record the results they found. Marie was a trained artist, so she also made sketches of the scientific equipment Antoine designed. Several of her drawings show the couple hard at work inside their lab.

The list of Antoine's accomplishments is long. He proved that fire and rust were both examples of oxidation, or chemical reactions that use oxygen. Antoine also showed that **respiration** was a form of oxidation inside living organisms.

Many of the Lavoisiers' experiments broke down **complex** substances into simpler ones. This work led to an amazing discovery. Sooner or later, they always ended up with substances that couldn't be broken down any farther. The Lavoisiers were discovering **elements**.

Soon, Antoine realized that water wasn't an element, which was what most scientists thought. Water was actually made of two elements—hydrogen and oxygen. Antoine also showed that air had a mixture of elements, although it was mostly nitrogen and oxygen.

Antoine's greatest discovery is now known as the *Law of Conservation of Matter*. He proved that elements aren't created or destroyed. Instead, a substance's molecules simply change forms during chemical reactions. This law is where all chemistry begins.

After Antoine's death, Marie kept their work alive. She published the results of their experiments. She also shared their research at meetings with other French scientists. Today, Antoine is considered one of history's greatest scientists.

Circle the letter of the best answer to each question below.

1. Antoine knew that water couldn't be an element because

 a. it contains both hydrogen and oxygen.

 b. it is a liquid.

 c. it doesn't have any atoms.

 d. it can't be burned.

2. Which of the following was not a discovery made by the Lavoisiers?

 a. the Law of the Conservation of Matter

 b. the elements

 c. atoms contain protons and electrons

 d. controlled experiments are good scientific tools

Write your answer on the lines below.

3. How did Marie use her artistic training in the lab?

 _____

4. Why does the author say that Marie Lavoisier was Antoine's greatest colleague?

 _____

 _____

5. During the 1800s, more and more women began attending college. What do you think would have happened if Marie Lavoisier had been able to attend college?

 _____

 _____

What's Next?

Artists play an important role in science. Ideas can be difficult to understand when they're explained only in words. A good illustration can quickly show why, where, or how something happens. Go to the library and browse through the science books to see just how important illustrations are.

The Gaia Hypothesis

cardiovascular system: the heart and blood vessels, which carry oxygen to cells and waste away from them

controversy: a heated debate about something in which people have different opinions

conscious: thinks about things and does things on purpose

automatically: done without thinking; not on purpose

ecologists: scientists who study how organisms live in and with their environment

Gaia was the Greek goddess of Earth.

One characteristic of living things is that they reproduce. If Earth is a living thing, how does it make copies of itself? Some people think human beings are the answer. As we travel farther into space, we might live on another planet. Could this be how Earth reproduces itself? Or is this idea just science fiction?

Is Earth a giant living organism?

In the early 1960s, a scientist named James Lovelock was looking for evidence of life on Mars. He began wondering why Earth had life but Mars didn't. Both planets were made of mostly the same chemicals. The difference was that Mars didn't have any chemical reactions, but Earth had plenty. Living things kept the chemicals on Earth mixing and changing.

Chemical reactions happen all the time inside living things. They're what keep you alive. Lovelock's thinking led him to form a hypothesis—Earth was alive, too. He called his idea the *Gaia Hypothesis*.

The systems inside your body control the chemicals that keep you alive. Too much or too little of certain chemicals can make you sick, or even kill you. The **cardiovascular system** is a good example. When you work hard, your muscles burn oxygen and create carbon dioxide. Your heart begins working faster to keep a healthy balance of these chemicals.

Earth's organisms keep the planet balanced in a similar way. Every plant and animal needs chemicals to live. The chemicals that an organism uses, though, are changed into different chemicals. For example, you change oxygen into carbon dioxide. Plants change carbon dioxide back into oxygen. Earth's chemicals are balanced by these kinds of living systems.

Lovelock saw that Earth had life because the living things worked together as a system that kept Earth balanced. He wrote a book about the Gaia Hypothesis. It created a **controversy**.

At first, many scientists thought Lovelock's idea was silly. Many cultures had myths about "Mother Earth," but it wasn't science. Did Lovelock mean that Earth was an animal? That Earth had a brain?

Lovelock argued that he wasn't saying Earth was **conscious**. Earth was more like plants or bacteria because its systems worked **automatically**. More scientists began to see that Lovelock's idea wasn't so crazy after all.

The Gaia Hypothesis has been around for more than 30 years. After a lot of debate and research, many scientists now agree that Earth is a kind of living system. **Ecologists** know that all organisms have roles in keeping Earth's systems in balance. Today, the Gaia Hypothesis is often called the *Gaia Theory*.

Circle the letter of the best answer to each question below.

1. Which of the following statements about the Gaia Hypothesis is true?

   a. Soon after Lovelock shared his idea, it was proven true.

   b. It states that Earth is a giant animal.

   c. Most scientists doubted it was true when they first heard the idea.

   d. All of the above

2. *Gaia* is

   a. Lovelock's middle name.

   b. a giant animal that lives in space.

   c. a kind of bacteria.

   d. the Greek goddess of Earth.

Write your answers on the lines below.

3. What are three things your body has in common with planet Earth?

   _____   _____   _____

4. What are three differences between human beings and planet Earth?

   _____   _____   _____

5. Do you agree with James Lovelock's idea? Why or why not?

   _____

   _____

Unifying Concepts and Processes

Review the steps in the scientific process (Chapter 1 Lesson 1). Explain how Lovelock's idea went from a question to a theory.

_____

_____

_____

_____

Dancing for Food

communicate: to share information

conclusion: a decision reached by reasoning

decode: to figure out the message of something in code

radar: a device that sends out radio waves; used to determine location and speed

When food is hard to come by, honeybees might travel as far as 10 miles from the hive.

Bees take into account the movement of the sun over the course of the day. For example, if a bee dances for several hours after finding food, the dance will change slightly as the sun moves across the sky or starts to set.

Von Frisch also wanted to know if bees could see colors. He fed them sugar water on a colored card. Then, he put that card among a bunch of gray cards. The bees flew right to the blue card, proving they could see color.

Do honeybees have a way to share information with each other?

Karl von Frisch was an Austrian zoologist who is best known for his work with honeybees. Von Frisch noticed that when a bee finds a good source of food or water, it returns to the hive. Soon, other bees from the hive travel to the same patch of flowers. Somehow, bees **communicate** with one another. Von Frisch set out to find out just how they do this.

Von Frisch observed that the bee that found the food source would dance when it returned to the hive. The bees that saw the dance were the ones that could find the food. Von Frisch came to the **conclusion** that the bees communicated by dancing, so that's what he began to study.

After spending a lot of time observing the bees' behavior, von Frisch found that the honeybees had two types of dances—the round dance and the waggle dance. The round dance was used when the food was close by. This dance didn't give the other bees specific directions. The waggle dance was used for food that was farther away. Von Frisch became even more excited when he discovered that the bees could actually give each other precise directions to find the food. The bees in the hive could learn how far away the food was and exactly how to find it.

Von Frisch found that bees use the sun as a compass. The directions they give in the waggle dance, when they wag their bodies quickly back and forth, give the position of the food by using the sun as a guide. Von Frisch spent so much time watching these dances that he could **decode** them perfectly.

Many other scientists of the time weren't convinced that von Frisch's theories were true. They thought that other explanations were possible. For example, how did von Frisch know that the bees weren't just following the scout back to the patch of flowers? Maybe there was a scent that the bee gave off that told the others where to look for food.

In 1973, von Frisch won the Nobel Prize—the highest honor for a scientist. It wasn't until 2005, though, that his hypothesis was finally proven true. Modern scientists watched the waggle dance in a glass beehive. They attached tiny **radar** to the bees so that they could follow them. Sure enough, von Frisch was right—the bees knew just where to go.

Circle the letter of the best answer to each question below.

1. Why didn't all scientists accept that von Frisch's findings were true?

   a. They thought his methods weren't very scientific.

   b. They didn't think bees were that smart.

   c. They believed that von Frisch was making up his results.

   d. They thought that there were other reasons the bees might have been able to find the food source.

2. Why do bees perform the waggle dance?

   a. to attract a mate

   b. to let other bees know where to find food

   c. to let other bees know that danger is near

   d. to keep other bees from finding their food

Write your answers on the lines below.

3. How is a round dance different from a waggle dance?

   _____

4. How do bees use the sun?

   _____

5. How did von Frisch come to the conclusion that bees communicate through dance?

   _____

   _____

6. Why do you think von Frisch used observation as his main method of investigation?

   _____

   _____

7. What might have been von Frisch's hypothesis when he began his study of honeybees?

   _____

   _____

Bringing Space Technology Down to Earth

How does space exploration help us in our everyday lives?

In 1957, the **Soviet Union** launched *Sputnik*, the first human-made **satellite**. Americans began worrying that they were being left behind in the race to explore space. The next year, the United States government formed the National Aeronautics and Space Administration, or NASA. NASA's goal was to get an American into space safely and quickly.

NASA's other important mission was to share its discoveries. A lot of new technologies were created as human beings raced into space. Today, we still benefit from NASA's research. Technologies that begin as part of the space program often end up being used every day here on Earth.

An astronaut floating inside a spacecraft doesn't want to get tangled in a bunch of cords. He or she needs tools that work without cords. Scientists designed cordless tools that used better, more powerful batteries. Today, hardware stores sell all sorts of cordless tools.

Astronauts also needed special boots to protect their feet. The soles of these boots were designed to absorb the shock that came from walking across the moon's rocky surface. Today, some athletic shoes have this same technology built into their soles.

You might be looking at a bit of space technology right now. The lenses of eyeglasses often have a special coating that makes them hard to scratch. This coating was first used to protect the delicate parts in spacecraft.

It takes a lot of energy to launch a spacecraft. The lighter it is, the less fuel it burns. Of course, spacecraft still need to be made of strong materials. Breaking through Earth's atmosphere takes a lot of force. NASA developed materials that are both strong and light. These materials are used now in a lot of sports equipment.

Launching a spacecraft creates incredible heat. Fireproof materials were invented that could stand up to these high temperatures. Today, the clothing of firefighters and racecar drivers are made of these materials.

One of your home's most important devices is a piece of space technology. Smoke detectors were used first in the Skylab space station in the 1970s. Today, they are found in every safe home.

Space travel helps us understand where we live in the universe. It's also a source of things that make life better right here on Earth.

Circle the letter of the best answer to the question below.

1. NASA stands for

   a. National Astronomy and Science Association

   b. New Academy of Space Activities

   c. National Aeronautics and Space Administration

   d. Nuclear and Space Association

Write your answers on the lines below.

2. Choose a technology from the selection. How was it used in space? How is it used on Earth?

   _____

   _____

   _____

3. NASA designed special thermometers that could measure the temperatures of stars. These thermometers read infrared waves in the spectrum to measure heat. They can take temperatures without having to touch things. How do you think these thermometers are being used today on Earth?

   _____

   _____

4. Freeze-drying, a space technology, removes all the moisture from a food item. Freeze-dried foods don't need to be refrigerated, and they can last for years. They are also very light. Hikers often bring freeze-dried foods on long hikes. Why is freeze-drying a good option for space travel?

   _____

   _____

What's Next?

Each year, NASA publishes a special report showing how space research is being used here on Earth. They call these new technologies *spinoffs*. This selection covered only a few examples of the hundreds of spinoffs NASA has developed. Do some research to find more examples. How many different space technologies do you use every day?

The End of the Dinosaurs

meteorites: space rocks that have fallen to the Earth's surface

extinct: no longer living or existing

climate: the average weather conditions in a specific place

crater: a bowl-shaped hole in a planet's surface, often caused by a meteorite

impact: a striking of two bodies against one another; a forceful collision

Scientists estimate that the meteorite that made the Chicxulub crater was about six miles wide. The energy that was released when it hit Earth was millions of times stronger than the strongest bomb human beings have ever exploded.

Dinosaurs aren't the only creatures that would have been affected by the meteorite. Scientists believe that more than three-quarters of all species were killed. The ones that survived were mostly smaller animals that could better adapt to all the changes that had taken place.

Why do many scientists believe that a huge meteorite caused the dinosaurs to disappear?

No one knows for certain why the dinosaurs that roamed Earth millions of years ago died out. One popular theory came about through the work of a father-and-son team of scientists—Luis and Walter Alvarez. In 1980, the Alvarezes were in Italy working on a geology project. They discovered something strange in the rocks there. It was a layer of a rare metal called *iridium*. Iridium exists in Earth's core, but there is very little near the surface. The Alvarezes did some more research and found this band of iridium around the world. Now, they just had to figure out how it got there.

Meteorites contain large amounts of iridium. The Alvarezes thought that an enormous meteorite might have hit Earth. The rock that contained the iridium was dated at 65 million years old. This is just about the time that dinosaurs became **extinct**.

The Alvarezes believed that when the meteorite hit Earth, it caused changes in the **climate**. The major explosion killed living things for miles and miles. It probably also triggered natural disasters, like wildfires, earthquakes, and tidal waves. They thought that the explosion sent huge amounts of smoke and dust into the atmosphere, which blocked the rays of the sun. The darkness and cooler temperatures caused many types of plants to die. When the plants began to die out, the dinosaurs that were herbivores, or plant-eaters, had nothing to eat. They, too, began to die out. The carnivorous, or meat-eating, dinosaurs used to eat the herbivores. Instead, they had to eat one another. Over time, their supply of food got smaller and smaller, until there were no dinosaurs left at all.

A giant **crater**, called *Chicxulub*, was found in the Yucatán peninsula of Mexico in the early 1990s. Scientists studied the rocks in the crater and found evidence that a huge **impact** happened there. The rocks also date back about 65 million years—the same time the iridium was deposited and the dinosaurs became extinct. This discovery helps support the Alvarezes' hypothesis.

Many scientists believe that the Chicxulub crater is where the giant meteorite hit Earth. Not all of them agree, though, that this caused the extinction of the dinosaurs. Even the scientists that do agree aren't sure exactly how it happened. Some believe that the Alvarezes' hypothesis makes sense. Others do not. Both sides realize there isn't enough information to prove it.

Use the words in the box to complete the sentences below.

crater	natural disasters	climate	iridium

1. _____ is a type of metal that is found in Earth's core and in meteorites.

2. Scientists think that the impact of a huge meteorite created a very large

   _____ .

3. It's likely that the meteorite caused different types of _____ .

4. Changes in _____ affected the dinosaurs.

Write your answers on the lines below.

5. What did the Alvarezes find that led them to come up with their hypothesis?

   _____

6. Why did the Alvarezes conclude that a giant meteorite hit Earth?

   _____

7. Why do you think that scientists disagree about the Alvarezes' idea of how dinosaurs became extinct?

   _____

   _____

8. Explain how scientists think a giant meteorite might have affected the food chain.

   _____

   _____

   _____

What's Next?

There are many ideas about why the dinosaurs became extinct. See how many you can find, either online or at the library. Which one makes the most sense to you? Which has the best support in the scientific community?

interact: to act on or affect one another

toxic: poisonous

precise: exact

Robots have practical uses in the home, too. Robotic vacuum cleaners can vacuum the house on their own. They have special sensors that keep them from running into walls and furniture.

Some robots are made to be companions for human beings. They have been used with the elderly and people who are disabled. These mechanical friends can speak and recognize voices. They can often do simple household tasks and even call for help if something seems to be wrong.

"A robot may not injure a human being, or, through inaction, allow a human being to come to harm." The First Law of Robotics —Isaac Asimov, writer and scientist

What role do robots play in the world today?

When most people picture robots, they think of something out of a science-fiction movie or novel. Robots aren't just a part of the future, though. Hundreds of thousands of them are hard at work right now all around the world. You might be surprised to find out just what these mechanical creatures can do.

A robot isn't just a machine. Like a machine, it has parts and a motor and can perform certain tasks. A robot is different, though. It can usually move, handle objects, and **interact** with its environment. A toy dog that can bark and wag its tail isn't a robot. What if it could chase a ball when you threw it, barked only at strangers, and wagged its tail when you gave it food? This dog definitely has the qualities of a robot.

Today, many robots are used for tasks that are dangerous or unpleasant for human beings. They can be used in labs to handle materials like blood, for example. Robots can clean **toxic** waste. In times of war, they can save lives. Robots have been used as scouts to locate bombs. They safely explode the bombs and make sure that no one gets hurt.

Robots can be sent places where it would be difficult or expensive to send human beings. A robot called *Jason Jr.* was used to explore the wreck of the *Titanic* more than 12,000 feet underwater. Robots are also useful space travelers. A robot spacecraft named *Galileo* orbited Jupiter for eight years and collected information about its atmosphere and moons. The radiation levels are 1,000 times stronger than what a human being could survive, so a robot was the perfect substitute.

Another common use for robots is factory work, or work that involves doing the same thing over and over. Human beings can get tired and make mistakes when they have to repeat things over a long period of time. Robots are very **precise**, and they never get tired. They can even work 24 hours a day. Work gets done quickly, which saves the company money.

Even doctors use robots. Today, they can help do certain types of surgery. In the future, robots will do surgery on their own, under the direction of a doctor. There's a good chance that if you can imagine a robot doing something, someone is already designing it.

Circle the letter of the best answer to the question below.

1. Robots are an important type of technology for human beings because

   a. they can save people time and money.

   b. they can do tasks that human beings can't do.

   c. they are smarter than human beings.

   d. Both a and b

Write **true** or **false** next to each statement below.

2. _____ Robots are becoming more common, but only a few hundred are in use today.

3. _____ All robots are machines, but not all machines are robots.

4. _____ Robots are able to interact with their environments.

5. _____ Inventors have not yet found a use for robots in times of war.

Write your answers on the lines below.

6. Name three ways that robots are used in society today.

   _____

   _____

7. What is a benefit of using robots to explore outer space or deep underwater?

   _____

8. Why would a factory choose to use a robot instead of a human being for a task like putting together car parts?

   _____

Unifying Concepts and Processes

Robots are replacing some factory workers. Could robots replace human beings in other jobs, too? Are they better suited to some types of work than others? Explain.

   _____

   _____

   _____

NAME _____

Review

Circle the letter of the best answer to each question below.

1. Antoine Lavoisier is called the "father of modern chemistry" because he

   a. performed carefully controlled experiments.

   b. discovered the Law of Conservation of Matter.

   c. discovered elements.

   d. all of the above

2. Honeybees communicate with each other by

   a. dancing.

   b. releasing a strong odor.

   c. stinging.

   d. None of the above

3. Why was NASA created?

   a. to help the Soviets

   b. to send human beings into space

   c. to repair *Sputnik*

   d. to build the International Space Station

4. Why was the layer of iridium that Luis and Walter Alvarez found important?

   a. because iridium was one of the dinosaurs' main sources of food

   b. because iridium is worth a lot of money

   c. because iridium is found only in space

   d. because iridium is not usually found near Earth's surface

Write your answers on the lines below.

5. Name two scientific ideas from ancient Greece that we know today are true.

   _____

   _____

6. What led to the Lavoisiers' discovery of the elements?

   _____

   _____

7. Explain the Gaia Hypothesis and give one reason to support it.

_____

_____

8. How did modern scientists prove that von Frisch's theories about bees were true?

_____

9. Give three examples of everyday items that use space technology.

_____

_____

10. Explain the Alvarezes' chain of events that started with a meteorite hitting Earth and led to the dinosaurs' extinction.

_____

_____

_____

11. Give one example of a machine. Then, describe how that same machine would be different if it were a robot.

_____

_____

Write **true** or **false** next to each statement below.

12. _____ Scientific ideas from the past aren't useful to today's scientists.

13. _____ Antoine Lavoisier's greatest colleague was his wife, Marie.

14. _____ All scientists believe the Gaia Hypothesis is true.

15. _____ The purpose of most robots is to be companions to human beings.

16. _____ Bees can give each other specific directions to food that is quite far away.

17. _____ Smoke detectors were first used in space.

18. _____ According to the Alvarezes, a giant meteor hit Earth and caused the extinction of the dinosaurs.

Circle the letter of the best answer to each question below.

1. The Law of the Conservation of Matter states that

    a. matter is destroyed at high temperatures.

    b. at very cold temperatures, atoms stop moving.

    c. molecules are the smallest pieces of matter.

    d. matter isn't created or destroyed.

2. Fire is an example of

    a. a chemical reaction.

    b. oxidation.

    c. fuel.

    d. Both a and b

3. Which of the following is not a part of Linnaeus's system of classifying living things?

    a. color

    b. genus

    c. species

    d. family

Write **true** or **false** next to each statement below.

4. _____ Atoms and molecules never stop moving.

5. _____ Fresh water is denser than salt water.

6. _____ Carnivores get the plant nutrients they need by eating herbivores.

7. _____ Worms are harmful to soil because they eat all the nutrients in it.

8. _____ Stalagmites and stalactites are made of hardened mud.

9. _____ It takes less energy to recycle aluminum than it does to create new aluminum.

10. _____ Clouds form when moisture in the air condenses around dust particles.

11. _____ The Hubble Space Telescope orbits the sun and sends images back to Earth.

12. _____ Hybrid cars use gasoline only to accelerate.

13. _____ MyPyramid shows that you should eat foods from only one category each day.

Draw a line to match each scientist or pair of scientists with their hypothesis.

14. Karl von Frisch   a. Everything is made of tiny particles called *atoms*.

15. Democritus   b. Earth is a giant, living organism.

16. Luis and Walter Alvarez   c. Water is not an element.

17. James Lovelock   d. Bees communicate by dancing.

18. Antoine and Marie Lavoisier   e. Dinosaurs became extinct when a meteorite hit Earth.

19. Place a check mark beside types of waves in the spectrum.

_____ gases   _____ light   _____ microwaves   _____ air   _____ x-rays

Write your answers on the lines below.

20. Bats and platypuses are both nocturnal animals. Explain how each finds prey in the dark.

_____

_____

21. Name something that is a system and something that is not a system.

System: _____   Nonsystem: _____

22. Explain why Earth is a system.

_____

23. A block of aluminum and a block of steel have the same volume but the aluminum has less mass. What does this tell you about aluminum compared to steel?

_____

24. Why are bar graphs and other graphic organizers helpful tools?

_____

25. What problem was Charles Goodyear trying to solve?

_____

26. Choose one of Newton's three laws of motion and give an example.

_____

27. Explain why light comes on when you flip a switch on the wall.

_____

_____

28. The distance to stars is measured in light years. Explain what a light year is.

_____

29. Name two ways in which carnivores and herbivores are different from one another.

_____

_____

30. Why are phytoplankton important to all forms of animal life on Earth?

_____

31. What is one role mangrove trees play in their ecosystem?

_____

32. How do icebergs form, and why don't they last forever?

_____

_____

33. Why does the moon appear to change shape?

_____

34. How does having an atmosphere affect a planet?

_____

35. Inside spacesuits are tubes that run water around the astronaut's body to keep it cool. How do you think this technology is being used on Earth?

_____

36. Why are CFLs more efficient than regular light bulbs?

_____

NAME _____

37. How do microwaves affect the molecules in a piece of food?

_____

38. Why do you need to drink water when you exercise?

_____

39. How can you tell which kinds of plastics can be easily recycled?

_____

40. What happens to the waste taken from nuclear power plants?

_____

41. Why were people in the 1800s getting ill when they drank water from the River Thames?

_____

42. Why are robots useful for exploring space?

_____

Complete each sentence below by choosing a word from the box.

particles	**collecting**	**variables**	**displace**
oxygen	**food chain**	**results**	**reflects**

43. Smoke is not a gas, it is _____ that are floating away from a fire.

44. Observing, experimenting, and _____ are methods of scientific investigation.

45. An experiment shouldn't have too many _____, or you might have trouble

figuring out why you got certain _____ .

46. An object placed in water will _____ its weight in water.

47. Every fire needs fuel, _____, and heat.

48. An orange shirt _____ orange light waves.

49. Phytoplankton are the lowest level of the marine _____.

Answer Key

Page 7

1. c
2. a
3. b
4. Possible answer: It's a statement that can be tested and proven right or wrong.
5. Possible answer: Sharing results lets other scientists check the experiment. They try to get the same results.
6. 2, 1, 3, 6, 5, 4

Page 9

1. b
2. d
3. a
4. Answers will vary.

Unifying Concepts and Processes

Possible answer: No. Scientists will use whatever method works best for their research. It doesn't matter what branch of science they are working in.

Page 11

1. c
2. Answers will vary.
3. Possible answer: A lock is a system. The key is the part that turns the lock so it will open or close.
4. Possible answer: The plastic or glass that protects the clock face could be missing, and the clock would still work. If the hands were missing, the clock would no longer tell what the time was.
5. Possible answers: School system—I'm a student. Family—I do chores. Soccer team—I help try to score goals.

Unifying Concepts and Processes

Possible answer: An ecosystem is a system, so every plant and animal is necessary, no matter how small. If one of them is missing, the ecosystem won't work as well.

Page 13

1. c
2. 8
3. worms, beetles
4. centipedes
5. termites
6. Possible answer: It let them compare how many of each insect they found.
7. The bugs ran away before the boys could count them.

8. Alex counted the insects that had been under the log. Austin put the log on a white sheet so he could count the rest of the insects before they escaped.

9. Possible answer: The boys looked under only one log. Different insects might be under other logs.

Page 15

1. c

2. d

3. Possible answer: She put the baking soda into the balloon so the reaction wouldn't happen until the balloon was on the bottle. The gas might have escaped, and the balloon wouldn't inflate.

4. If you change more than one variable at a time, you won't know which one caused a change in the results.

5. Possible answer: Baker's yeast will react with vinegar to create a gas and inflate the balloon.

6. Answers will vary

Page 17

1. b

2. d

3. a

4. Possible answer: Rubber wasn't a useful material because it melted at high temperatures and froze at low temperatures.

5. Possible answer: It took him a long time to find a solution to the problem. He had to do many experiments.

6. The acid ruined it.

7. Possible answer: They let him try out different ideas. He could easily see which ideas worked and which ideas did not.

Page 19

1. c

2. b

3. c

4. Possible answer: Weight measures how strongly gravity pulls down on an object. Each planet has different amounts of gravity, so the weight changes.

5. Possible answer: Block B is made of a denser material than Block A.

Page 20

1. c

2. d

3. a

4. d

5. c

Answer Key

Page 21

6. They use different methods because not all methods would work well for all types of investigations.

7. question   hypothesis   share results

8. A bicycle has many parts that work together.

9. Possible answers: a plate, a stick

10. Possible answers: He had a lot of patience. He performed many experiments until he found a solution to a problem. His discovery happened by accident, but he was paying close attention and realized what had happened.

11. Weight measures how much gravity pulls on an object, and mass is how many kilograms something has.

12. false

13. false

14. true

15. true

16. false

17. true

Page 23

1. 3
2. 1
3. 2
4. 3
5. 2
6. 1
7. reaction
8. rest
9. Force
10. It will change speed or direction. Possible example: A car is driving down the street when it is hit by another car. It is now heading in another direction.
11. The wagon will be moving faster, according to Newton's second law. It is lighter and has less mass, so the force you are using will make it move more quickly.

Page 25

1. d
2. b
3. c
4. Possible answer: The apple on the left shrank when some of its molecules changed to gases. The molecules stayed inside the sealed jar, though, so the weight didn't change.

5. Possible answers: heat, pressure

6. chemical

Page 27

1. b

2. c

3. a

4. c

5. Molecules are always moving, so the food coloring molecules and water molecules mixed together overnight.

Page 29

1. b

2. true

3. true

4. false

5. false

6. Possible answer: Your weight displaces some of the water in the tub. The water has to have someplace to go, so the level in the tub rises.

7. Possible answer: You could put both objects in a bucket of water and see whether one floats better than the other.

8. so that it will sink in the freshwater

Unifying Concepts and Processes

Possible answer: the type of jar used; It would take more buoyancy force to get a heavier jar to float.

Page 31

1. b

2. d

3. c

4. chemical reaction

5. Possible answer: Gas fuels don't contain solids. There is no soot to give the flame an orange or yellow color, so the flame is blue.

6. Possible answer: Oxidation is a chemical reaction that uses oxygen. Fire occurs when oxygen mixes with other gases and burns.

7. Wax, the wick

Answer Key

Page 33

1. b
2. d
3. d

Unifying Concepts and Processes

Possible answer: The filament wire is part of a circuit because electricity flows through it. When the filament breaks, it creates an open circuit.

Page 35

1. b
2. c
3. d
4. Possible answer: A banana is yellow because every color but yellow is absorbed. Only yellow light waves reflect off its surface and reach the eye.
5. They are all types of waves in the spectrum.

Page 36

1. a
2. c
3. d
4. a
5. chemical
6. Possible answers: kerosene; wood
7. closed; open
8. liquid, solid, gas

Page 37

9. Possible answer: An ice cube can change into water.
10. The food coloring turned the water green instead of staying concentrated at the bottom of the glass.
11. The salt water had greater density, so it had greater buoyancy force.
12. Things are very buoyant in the Dead Sea.
13. A blue box absorbs all colors except blue. It reflects blue light waves.
14. force
15. accelerated
16. displace
17. physical
18. reflect
19. chemical

20. fuel

21. current

Page 39

1. In the classification system, a kingdom is more (<u>general</u>, specific) than an order.

2. Scientific names are (<u>the same</u>, different) all around the world.

3. The scientific name for (dogs, <u>human beings</u>) is *Homo sapiens*.

4. A flea, a tree, a rabbit, and a mushroom are all examples of (genuses, <u>organisms</u>).

5. A botanist is a scientist who studies (<u>plants</u>, animal behavior).

6. Possible answer: The old method was too long and complicated.

7. Possible answer: It helps scientists study things in the natural world and talk about their findings.

8. *Panthera*; *tigris*

9. They have the same genus.

10. No, every animal has a different name. No one would know which animal people were talking about otherwise.

Page 41

1. b

2. false

3. true

4. true

5. false

6. They eat herbivores, which are plant-eating animals.

7. an omnivore

8. Possible answers: Carnivores have sharp, pointy teeth for tearing meat. Herbivores have very long small intestines because plant materials are harder to digest.

Unifying Concepts and Processes

Possible answers: It makes the animals easier to study. Scientists can look for similarities and differences between animals.

Page 43

1. c

2. b

3. false

4. true

5. true

6. false

7. Phytoplankton are at the bottom of the marine food chain.

8. Possible answer: Plants don't grow in some parts of the desert, so there are few animals. Plankton aren't found in some parts of the ocean, so there are very few marine animals there.

Unifying Concepts and Processes

Possible answer: bacteria that drift through the ocean

Page 45

1. a

2. c

3. Possible answer: A platypus has receptors in its bill to locate prey.

4. Possible answer: The heart carries oxygen through the body. The platypus's slow heart rate uses less oxygen, so it can stay underwater longer.

Unifying Concepts and Processes

Possible answer: The platypus has characteristics of both mammals and reptiles. It shows scientists that mammals and reptiles might have evolved from the same animal.

Page 47

1. c

2. b

3. Nocturnal animals are active at night, and diurnal animals are active during the day.

4. Possible answer: Echolocation is when a high-pitched sound hits an object and bounces back. This helps bats hunt at night because they don't have to be able to see their prey.

5. Owls have become nocturnal creatures. Many of the animals they hunt are nocturnal.

6. Possible answer: Fewer animals are awake at night, so the eggs and the babies have a better chance of surviving.

Page 49

1. d

2. b

3. It is a community of living things.

4. Possible answers: They keep the land from eroding too quickly. They can also keep it from flooding.

5. The roots of the trees protect the young animals.

6. Mangrove trees have large root systems that are above the ground. The roots get covered in salt water at high tide, but the trees do not.

Page 51

1. d

2. a

3. b

4. They fertilize it with their castings. They also make tunnels, which let air flow through the soil.

5. They eat the soil, sand, leaves, and grass clippings.

Unifying Concepts and Processes

Possible answer: They make the soil healthier for plants. Plants are at the bottom of the food chain, so all other forms of life depend on them.

Page 52

1. a

2. b

3. b

4. d

5. This lets them communicate and share information.

6. Species

7. omnivores

Page 53

8. Phytoplankton are plants, and zooplankton are animals.

9. The strong acids break down the chunks of meat and kill the bacteria in it.

10. pollution; Earth's warming climate

11. Possible answer: It lays eggs.

12. Possible answer: They make high-pitched sounds that bounce off objects, like insects, so that the bats can figure out their location even in the dark.

13. Possible answers: They live in the desert, and it is too hot to be active during the day. There are fewer predators out at night.

14. Earthworms leave castings that are rich in nutrients in the soil. They also make tunnels that let air and water flow through the soil.

15. draw a line to d

16. draw a line to e

17. draw a line to g

18. draw a line to c

19. draw a line to f

20. draw a line to a

21. draw a line to b

Page 54

1. a

2. b

3. the light

4. Possible answer: Pupils get smaller in brighter light.

5. Possible answer: Pupils get smaller in brighter light.

6. Possible answer: Yes. They did an experiment, but part of the experiment was observing how eyes react to light.

7. Possible answer: They provide habitat for animals, and their roots filter the water.

8. Possible answer: It should be dark, moist, and have something like leaves or grass for food.

Page 55

9. fuel, oxygen, and heat

10. Possible answer: The old way was too complicated and confusing.

11. Possible answer: Because they eat different things.

12. Possible answers: Because phytoplankton are at the bottom of the marine food chain.

13. check mark next to: squirrel, dishwasher

14. Possible answer: For every action, there is an equal and opposite reaction.

15. Electricity will flow through a closed circuit, but not an open circuit.

16. The more (<u>atoms</u>, volume) something has the more mass it will have.

17. Steam is an example of water that has gone through a (chemical, <u>physical</u>) change.

18. When you put a battery into a device, it becomes part of the (current, <u>circuit</u>).

19. Light waves and radio waves are part of the (<u>spectrum</u>, air).

20. A predator is not a(n) (<u>herbivore</u>, carnivore).

21. Like all plants, phytoplankton emit (carbon dioxide, <u>oxygen</u>).

22. To escape the heat of the day, many desert animals are (<u>nocturnal</u>, diurnal.)

23. true

24. false

25. false

26. false

Page 57

1. c

2. d

3. false

4. true

5. true

6. false

7. Calving is when a chunk of ice breaks off an ice sheet or glacier and forms an iceberg.

8. Possible answer: Wind, waves, and weather break icebergs into smaller and smaller pieces until they are gone.

9. Possible answer: Tabular. These icebergs are flat and horizontal, like a table. The other iceberg shapes would be too hard to build things on.

Page 59

1. d
2. b
3. ceiling
4. groundwater
5. ground
6. calcium
7. Possible answer: Water drips slowly from the ceiling of a cave. It contains calcium. When the water dries up, the calcium is left behind. Over time, it forms stalactites.
8. Possible answer: These two substances probably contain calcium or another, similar mineral.

Page 61

1. c
2. a
3. They are both metals. Gold is found by itself in nature, but aluminum is always combined with something else.
4. Possible answer: Aluminum is strong but light. It is used in the body of an airplane because it can stand up to wind and bad weather.
5. It is better to recycle them. It uses less energy to recycle aluminum than it does to make new aluminum.

Unifying Concepts and Processes

A cheaper, easier way was found to separate aluminum from other substances. It was no longer as rare.

Page 63

1. c
2. b
3. c
4. The smoke provided dust particles for water to condense around.
5. Possible answer: When temperatures drop, moisture in the air condenses on things. At night it gets cooler, so moisture condenses on the grass.

Unifying Concepts and Processes

Possible answer: The cloud drops snow or hail to the ground.

Page 65

1. c
2. b

3. gibbous

4. sun

5. cycle

6. orbit

7. A waxing gibbous moon appears before a full moon, and a waning gibbous moon appears after a full moon.

8. The moon appears to change shape because the amount of the lit side you can see changes as the moon orbits Earth.

Page 67

1. c

2. b

3. c

4. Possible answer: Earth and Venus both have atmospheres. Earth and Venus are both terrestrial planets.

5. Wind moves through atmospheres; Mercury has very little atmosphere.

6. Possible answer: Life can exist only where water is a liquid. Earth's temperatures keep water as a liquid most of the time. On the other planets, water is always steam or ice.

Page 69

1. a

2. b

3. true

4. false

5. false

6. true

7. Possible answer: Galaxies are shaped like water swirling down a drain. This tells scientists that something with very strong gravity—like a black hole—is pulling stars into each galaxy's center.

8. Possible answer: Lights on Earth can make it hard to use a telescope that is on the ground. Hubble orbits Earth, so these lights aren't a problem.

Page 70

1. c

2. b

3. c

4. a

5. d

Page 71

6. It is a strong material, and it won't rust.

7. Possible answer: Air currents carry moisture high into Earth's atmosphere. The cooler temperatures cause moisture to condense around dust particles and form water droplets. The water droplets collect together and form a cloud.

8. They are huge planets that are always frozen because they are so far from the sun.

9. They are made of freshwater, which is less dense than salt water, so they float.

10. Answers will vary.

11. Organisms need liquid water in order to live, and Earth is the only planet that has it.

12. Possible answer: Hubble has been used to study black holes.

13. glacier

14. evaporates

15. mined

16. condenses

17. galaxies

Page 73

1. c

2. b

3. Possible answers: They can be a source of drinking water, control flooding, and irrigate farms.

4. Possible answers: It doesn't cause pollution, and it is a renewable source of energy.

5. Possible answers: They are made of different materials. They are used for protection and food storage.

6. They block the flow of water, which builds up and forms a pool.

Page 75

1. d

2. b

3. It is pure oxygen. The air on Earth contains a lot of nitrogen, too.

4. Possible answers: Spacesuits protect astronauts from extreme temperatures and micrometeoroids.

5. Possible answer: They are able to leave the spaceship to explore and to make repairs.

6. Some of the materials used in them are the same.

Page 77

1. b

2. d

3. nervous

4. unconscious

5. Possible answers: Having a cavity filled is not major surgery. The patient would experience pain in only one small area.

6. Possible answers: There are more surgeries done today. People don't have to experience as much pain because of anesthesia.

Answer Key

7. The anesthesiologist gives the patient anesthesia and monitors the patient afterward.

Page 79

1. d
2. c
3. true
4. false
5. false
6. true
7. Possible answers: Hybrid cars use less gasoline. They pollute less.
8. Possible answer: On the highway, hybrid cars use more gasoline. In cities, they stop and start more often, so they use more electric power, recharge their batteries, and pollute less.

Unifying Concepts and Processes

Possible answer: When hybrid cars are already moving, they don't need much energy to keep moving. The gas engine is used then because it won't need to burn much gas, and it won't create very much pollution.

Page 81

1. b
2. c
3. true
4. false
5. true
6. true
7. false
8. true
9. Possible answer: Yes. CFLs will save money for the people who use them. CFLs also cause less pollution because they use less energy.

Page 83

1. a
2. d
3. true
4. false
5. true
6. false
7. Possible answer: They would probably be much smaller.

8. Possible answers: The farmer can track specific information about each cow. Human beings don't have to be there for any part of the milking process.

9. Possible answers: They might not know if there was a problem with one of the cows.

Page 85

1. b

2. d

3. Microwaves cause water molecules to move around quickly. The movement cooks the food.

4. The ceramic plate became hot because of the food's heat, not because of the microwaves.

5. She should use a regular oven, or else the bread will not have a crusty outer layer.

Unifying Concepts and Processes

Possible answer: Yes. Even though his discovery was an accident, he was smart to try to figure out why the candy bar had melted and how he could use this information.

Page 86

1. b

2. d

3. c

4. a

5. Possible answers: They irrigate farms and provide drinking water.

6. It doesn't cause pollution, and it is a renewable resource.

Page 87

7. Human beings exhale carbon dioxide. It would be dangerous for them to breathe in the carbon dioxide, so it has to be removed from the spacesuit.

8. Possible answer: People could handle surgery better. They weren't as worried about pain. It also made more serious types of surgery possible.

9. Burning fossil fuels creates air pollution and is one cause of global warming.

10. Hybrids use gas only when the car is already moving, otherwise they use electricity.

11. CFLs contain mercury, which is a poison.

12. Possible answer: They have given the farmers more flexibility in their lives. They have saved farmers time and money.

13. The food absorbs microwaves. This causes their molecules to move around quickly, which cooks the food.

14. true

15. false

16. false

17. true

18. true

Answer Key

Page 89

1. b
2. a
3. d
4. sweat, waste, breathing
5. You feel thirsty.
6. Possible answer: Lost water needs to be replaced. Caffeine in pop will make your body lose even more water. Your body uses up water when it breaks down the sugars in the juice.
7. Possible answer: When you exercise, you lose a lot of water through sweating. You must replace that water because your body needs it to work well.

Page 91

1. dark green spinach
2. low-fat strawberry yogurt
3. an orange
4. whole-wheat toast with peanut butter
5. a piece of lean chicken
6. to show people how to eat well and stay healthy
7. It stands for foods that don't fall into the other categories. It is small because you shouldn't eat much of these foods.
8. 3 ounces
9. They build strong bones and help you grow.
10. Because exercise is an important part of being healthy.

Page 93

1. b
2. c
3. Possible answer: Sick people cough or sneeze viruses onto their hands, and then they touch things. Other people come along and touch the same things. If they don't wash their hands, they can get the virus inside their bodies.
4. Possible answer: There are too many different cold viruses to find a cure for them all. They also evolve quickly, so new ones are always developing.
5. Because colds are caused by viruses, not bacteria.

Page 95

1. d
2. d
3. Plastic is durable.
4. Possible answer: Plastic can be burned to create energy.

5. Possible answer: Plastic can be recycled or reused. Otherwise, it just sits forever in a landfill.

6. Possible answer: Plastic bags. They take a lot less energy to make, but I would also be sure to recycle them.

Page 97

1. b

2. c

3. c

4. Because cod was in danger of disappearing completely.

5. No one knows for sure.

6. Possible answers: They took too much cod from the ocean in a short period of time. They also damaged the marine ecosystems.

7. They salted it and dried it.

Page 99

1. b

2. b

3. c

4. Possible answer: It is a bad idea. Nuclear fuel and waste are too dangerous. It is better to try to make energy with solar or wind power because they are much safer.

Page 101

1. c

2. b

3. d

4. pollution in the Thames; hot weather

5. Possible answer: People didn't drink water from the ocean, so the waste could be dumped there safely. People do eat fish from the ocean, so the pollution could still make them sick.

Unifying Concepts and Processes

Possible answer: The dirty water would flow downstream to the next city and make the people there sick.

Page 102

1. b

2. b

3. c

4. d

5. 1; 2

6. Wash your hands often, and don't touch your face.

7. People are different ages and have different levels of activity.

Answer Key

8. Because you should eat less of these foods.

9. to digest food, to get rid of waste products

10. sweating, going to the bathroom

11. Possible answer: Bacteria and viruses can both make people sick. Bacteria are living things, but scientists aren't sure whether viruses are alive or not.

12. Because there have been other changes in their ecosystem. Another type of fish may now be one of the top predators in the food chain.

13. Possible answer: Nuclear fuel and nuclear waste are radioactive.

14. Possible answer: Nuclear energy doesn't cause global warming.

15. Drinking unclean water can make people sick.

16. The most nutritious fruits and vegetables are the ones that are the (most, least) colorful.

17. Cold viruses (evolve, infect) the area between the nose and throat.

18. Plastic is made from (gasoline, petroleum).

19. (Technology, Trawlers) damaged the marine ecosystems where cod lived.

20. Atomic energy is (an alternative, a solution) to fossil fuels.

21. A (bacteria, cholera) epidemic in London was caused by dirty drinking water.

Page 105

1. a

2. d

3. true

4. true

5. He believed that Earth and the planets revolved around the sun.

6. He placed it in water. Then, he placed a piece of gold of the same size in water. The amount of water that overflowed was not the same for both pieces, so he knew the crown wasn't pure gold.

Unifying Concepts and Processes

Possible answer: Scientists build on each other's work. If the ancient Greeks hadn't shared their knowledge, then other scientists would have to learn for themselves all the things the Greeks already knew.

Page 107

1. a

2. c

3. She made drawings of Antoine's science equipment.

4. Possible answer: Marie helped Antoine with all of his experiments. She also made sure others learned about his discoveries after he died.

5. Possible answer: If Marie had been able to attend college, other scientists would have known she was educated. They would have accepted her as a scientist.

Page 109

1. c

2. d

3. Possible answers: They are both systems. They both use oxygen. They both contain water.

4. Possible answers: Earth is much bigger than I am. Earth can't reproduce. Earth doesn't have blood.

5. Possible answer: Yes. Earth doesn't look like any plants and animals that we know of, but it is a living system that uses chemical reactions.

Unifying Concepts and Processes

Possible answer: Lovelock asked why there was life on Earth. He made a hypothesis: "Earth is a living organism." He used observation to test his hypothesis. He concluded that his research proved the hypothesis. He shared his results with the scientific community. Other scientists tested his hypothesis. Many of them also found his hypothesis to be true, so the Gaia Hypothesis became the Gaia Theory.

Page 111

1. d

2. b

3. The round dance is used for food that is nearby. It doesn't give specific directions.

4. Bees use the sun as a guide when they give the position of a food source.

5. Possible answer: He observed a bee find food and return to the hive and dance. After seeing the dance, the other bees knew where the food was.

6. Possible answer: It would have been difficult to use other methods of investigation. Observing allowed him to get the information he needed.

7. Honeybees dance to tell other bees where food is located.

Page 113

1. c

2. Possible answer: Cordless tools were used in space so that astronauts didn't get tangled in the cords. On Earth, they are used so people can do work in places where there aren't outlets.

3. Possible answer: They can take a person's temperature without having to stick a thermometer into his or her mouth.

4. Possible answer: Freeze-dried foods are lighter, so less energy is used to carry the food into space. They also don't need to be kept cold, so the spacecraft doesn't need a refrigerator.

Page 115

1. Iridium

2. crater

3. natural disasters

4. climate

5. They found a layer of a rare metal called *iridium*.

6. Because iridium is not found near Earth's surface, but it is found in meteorites.

7. Possible answer: Other explanations are possible. There isn't enough evidence to prove that the other explanations couldn't be true.

8. The meteorite caused changes in the climate that made the plants die out. Dinosaurs that were herbivores didn't have anything to eat, so they died, too. The carnivores had to eat each other, until no dinosaurs were left.

Page 117

1. d

2. false

3. true

4. true

5. false

6. Possible answers: They can handle dangerous materials. They can explode bombs. They can explore deep underwater.

7. It's less expensive than using human beings, and it keeps people out of dangerous situations.

8. Robots are very precise, and they never get tired.

Unifying Concepts and Processes

Answers will vary.

Page 118

1. d

2. a

3. b

4. d

5. Possible answers: All things are made of tiny particles called *atoms*. Earth is not at the center of the universe.

6. Many of the Lavoisiers' experiments broke substances down into simpler substances. The substances that couldn't be broken down any further were the elements.

Page 119

7. Possible answer: Lovelock believed that Earth was a giant living organism. Like other living things, it uses chemical reactions and has many systems that work together.

8. They attached tiny radar to the bees so they could track them.

9. Answers will vary. Possible answers: smoke detectors; lenses that can't be scratched; cordless tools

10. A large meteorite hit Earth and caused a change in the climate. Plants were not able to survive the change. Dinosaurs that were herbivores didn't have anything to eat, so they died, too. The carnivores had to eat each other, until dinosaurs were extinct.

11. Possible answer: A toaster is a machine. A toaster that can butter the toast once it is done and put it on a plate would be a robot.

12. false

13. true

14. false

15. false

16. true

17. true

18. true

Page 120

1. d

2. d

3. a

4. true

5. false

6. true

7. false

8. false

9. true

10. true

11. false

12. false

13. false

Page 121

14. line connecting to d

15. line connecting to a

16. line connecting to e

17. line connecting to b

18. line connecting to c

19. check mark next to light; microwaves; x-rays

20. Bats make sounds and listen to how they echo. The way the sound echoes tells a bat where its prey is. Platypuses sense electricity in the water that was caused by movement.

21. Possible answer: computer; piece of paper

Answer Key

22. Possible answer: Earth has many different ecosystems that all work together.

23. Aluminum is less dense than steel.

24. Possible answer: Graphic organizers are an easy way to look at data and compare facts.

25. Goodyear wanted to make rubber that wouldn't melt or freeze easily.

26. Possible answer: Third Law of Motion; A cup sits on a table because the table pushes back at the cup with equal force.

Page 122

27. Possible answer: An electrical circuit runs from the switch, to the light, and back to the switch. Flipping on the switch closes the circuit so electricity flows to the bulb and lights it.

28. A lightyear is the distance light travels in one year.

29. Possible answer: Carnivores eat meat, but herbivores eat only plants. Carnivores have stronger acids in their stomachs to help them digest raw meat.

30. Possible answer: Phytoplankton produce a large percentage of Earth's oxygen.

31. Possible answer: Mangrove trees provide habitat for many animals.

32. Icebergs form when large chunks of ice break away from glaciers or ice sheets. Wind and weather break up icebergs into smaller pieces, and heat melts them.

33. We see changing amounts of the moon's lit side as it orbits Earth each month.

34. Possible answer: An atmosphere holds in the sun's warmth, and it is where wind is created.

35. Possible answer: Firefighters could wear this technology inside burning buildings.

36. Possible answer: They last longer, and they use less energy.

Page 123

37. Microwaves cause the atoms and molecules to move faster, so the food gets hotter.

38. You need to replace the water your body loses through sweat.

39. Look for a triangle with a 1 or 2 inside it.

40. Possible answer: It is buried deep underground, where it is still dangerous for thousands of years.

41. Possible answer: The river water was polluted and contained bacteria that made them sick.

42. Possible answer: Exploring space is dangerous, so using robots means that human beings don't have to be at risk.

43. particles

44. collecting

45. variables; results

46. displace

47. oxygen

48. reflects

49. food chain